CREATING
A CUSTOMER
FOCUSED
COMPANY

CREATING A CUSTOMER FOCUSED COMPANY

25 Proven Customer Service Strategies

IAN LINTON

FINANCIAL TIMES

PITMAN PUBLISHING

PITMAN PUBLISHING
128 Long Acre, London WC2E 9AN

A Division of Longman Group Limited

First published in 1994

© Ian Linton 1994

British Library Cataloguing in Publication Data
A CIP catalogue record for this book can be obtained from the British Library.

ISBN 0 273 60711 1

3 5 7 9 10 8 6 4 2

Typeset by Northern Phototypesetting Co. Ltd, Bolton
Printed and bound in Great Britain by
Biddles Ltd, Guildford and King's Lynn

*The Publishers' policy is to use paper manufactured
from sustainable forests.*

CONTENTS

INTRODUCTION

Customer service has become one of the key issues facing businesses, yet many companies pay it no more than lip-service. Changing the name on the door from complaints department to customer service is not sufficient because customer service simply becomes another method of handling complaints. Customer service is a practical process that involves the whole company. As the title of this book suggests, customer focus not customer service is the main issue.

Customer service suggests a product or service that is delivered, customer focus is an attitude that permeates the whole company. It suggests that every employee at every level is focused on customer needs, whether they deliver service or not. Customer focus begins with an understanding of the customer and permeates all the business processes that impact on the customer. While many companies limit their customer service programmes to direct customer-facing activities, there are a wide variety of business programmes that can be utilised to improve relations with the customer.

The book looks at the many different ways in which a company can help to meet its customers' needs – from making it easier for customers to place orders to developing customised products and services designed specifically for a customer. Although early customer service programmes concentrated on customer handling techniques – face to face, telephone and letters, the emphasis in this book is firmly on business programmes that can be used to develop relations at the right level.

The majority of programmes in this book are self-contained. They can be put into action by a management team with varying levels of resource and investment requirement. To help identify whether programmes are appropriate, each chapter contains a list of business scenarios that can be compared with your own business objectives.

The programmes also contain action guides that describe the main decisions and actions that should be reviewed to implement the programme. The more general programmes such as building a team or leading from the top include a wide range of tasks and implementation guidelines. Wherever possible, the programmes contain examples of best practice from a number of different companies and describe some of the issues they faced in implementing the programmes.

1

OVERVIEW

LEADING FROM THE TOP

This chapter looks at the role of the senior executive and examines the key management actions needed for the development of a customer focused organisation. It explains how the strategic customer focus decisions need to be taken by a senior executive team and outlines the risks and opportunities that should be assessed before committing an organisation to customer focus. It shows that there may be risks in not pursuing a customer focused strategy, allowing competitors to gain ground, but there are equal risks in pursuing a form of customer focus that puts considerable strain on an organisation's resources. The resource requirements change at each stage of customer focus and senior executives need to develop a policy for developing the right customer focus team. Issues such as skills development and investment need to be carefully considered.

Executives must also set easily measured standards that enable performance to be monitored and ensure the highest standards of quality. To achieve new standards, it may be necessary to transform the culture of an organisation; this requires vision and strong leadership, and senior executives will play a vital role. It is also important for senior executives to build good working because this demonstrates serious commitment to customer focus. New service development may be an important element in a customer focus strategy, and senior executives must review the risks and implications. Decisions must also be taken about the benefits and risks of working with third parties. Third parties may fill gaps in a company's own resources, but they should only be used if they can provide a quality service that will contribute to overall customer satisfaction.

BUILDING CUSTOMER TEAMS

The importance of building effective teams within your organisation and with your suppliers and distributors is explained in this chapter. It shows how customer focus depends on the performance of staff who are in direct contact with your customers and staff who provide essential customer support services. The members of the team vary from business to business so it is important to select a team that mirrors your customers' requirements. Many members of staff may not realise the importance of their contribution to customer satisfaction, so you need to make a positive effort to raise awareness of customer focus and build the commitment of all staff to its success. Developing customer focus standards and operating customer care training programmes help to improve staff performance in areas that are critical to success. You can also support your staff by improving or automating key customer services such as call reception, so freeing staff to deliver higher standards of personal service.

The role of the salesforce will change in a customer focus environment from 'hunter to farmer'. As they are the primary link with your customers, it is essential that they are trained in new customer service skills and receive full support from the rest of the customer team. Motivation and incentive programmes can be utilised to improve the performance of the customer team, but it is essential that the programmes are structured to reflect long-term customer requirements rather than tactical sales achievements. Finally, all the steps outlined in this chapter can be applied to the development of customer focus through your suppliers and distributors. They play an important role in building complete customer satisfaction and their contribution must be encouraged.

CUSTOMER RESEARCH

This chapter explains how to use information about your customers to assess the potential and likely contribution of customer focus. By analysing your sales and customer information you can build a profile of your customers' business and see how customer focus could best help them. The process may be as simple as identifying your largest customers and building close working relationships to protect the business. Pressures on your customers' supply position may encourage them to pursue closer ties, while a close study of their requirements enables you to identify the key factors that determine the direction of customer focus. Published surveys and other forms of research will provide a firm basis for developing a customer focus programme.

Competitive threats may make it necessary for you to strengthen customer focus, but there may be barriers if your customers' attitudes towards your competitors are more positive. By understanding your customers' strategies, their markets and their attitudes you can help to create the right environment for customer focus communications. You also need to assess your own strengths – how important are your products or your technical skills?

FOCUSING STAFF ON YOUR CUSTOMERS

'Put Yourself in Their Shoes' is a programme that helps staff understand customers by directly relaying customer comments to 'back-room staff'. The customer comments represent common problems in customer relations and encourage the staff to recognise their customers' concerns and take action. Action programmes should be put into place to improve performance and there should be a basis for measuring progress and comparative performance. The programme enables customer focus to be introduced throughout an organisation and helps to raise standards of customer service.

SETTING CUSTOMER FOCUS STANDARDS

This chapter shows how high standards of customer care are essential to building customer satisfaction and loyalty at local level and looks at the different ways in which customer care can be delivered. Customer focus panels, for example, help suppliers identify their customers' expectations and the chapter shows how these expectations can be used to develop customer focus standards which can contribute to consistent standards of customer care.

IMPROVING CONVENIENCE FOR CUSTOMERS

This chapter looks at ways of improving convenience for the customer and shows how companies in the retail sector have used factors such as longer opening hours, more convenient locations, better parking or public transport links and integration of leisure and shopping activities to make shopping a more convenient experience. The same principles can be applied to business and service industries by building closer working relationships and making it easier for customers to do business. In many cases, new technology can be used to improve aspects of convenience or to launch new services that help attract a different audience.

TALKING DIRECT TO CUSTOMERS

The ability to communicate with customers on an individual basis is important to a customer focused company. Tailored communications enable a company to address individual customer concerns and make offers to match their precise needs. Direct marketing is the main communications technique; customer information is held on a database and enhanced to provide a detailed picture of individual purchasing patterns. Groups of customers with similar purchasing potential can be selected for individual communications that are more effective than broadcast advertising.

ALIGNING SERVICES TO CUSTOMER NEEDS

This chapter explains the importance of customising support material and outlines the benefits to companies supplying both products and services. Using the example of local travel agents, it explains why individual outlets should be treated separately and provided with customised support packages, rather than uniform programmes. The chapter then explains how Speedwing Training researched the needs of individual travel agents as a basis for developing a training communications programme and customising their training services to the needs of individual branches.

SIMPLIFYING CUSTOMERS' BUSINESS PROCESSES

This chapter describes a number of ways in which companies strengthen relationships with customers by simplifying the customers' business processes. Partnership can be used to differentiate products and services that are otherwise subject to stringent price negotiation. To support the launch of a new product or service that has a low level of awareness and understanding in the market-place, companies can undertake joint market development projects. Logistics is a key factor in reducing the overall cost of production and improving standards of customer service. Logistics partnership can help partners improve performance. Fleet management is an example of a specific partnership service that can help customers attack problems on the balance sheet or improve customer service. Technology can help to build effective relationships with distributors and improve local customer service by achieving higher levels of consistency.

CUSTOMER CONTACT STRATEGIES

Regular communication with decision makers is essential to the success of customer focus. However, the communications programme must be based on carefully researched information needs. A communications audit can help you to assess attitudes towards your company and provides the basis for planning a communications strategy. Direct marketing can be used to ensure that individual decision makers receive the information they need, while product and technical updates ensure that your customers are kept fully informed on your technical performance. Regular briefings on corporate and financial developments build confidence and ensure that your company is regarded as a stable supplier. It is also important to assess customer attitudes to your performance and discuss improvement programmes through a series of regular team progress meetings. Large account teams can become unwieldy, but an account team manual will help to keep both parties informed about each other.

COURTESY SERVICES

The use of courtesy services such as courtesy cars is helping companies to increase customer satisfaction by reducing inconvenience for customers. The principle can also be applied to other sectors where customers can be inconvenienced when a product is under repair. A courtesy programme should be simple to administer for both customer and manufacturer and should demonstrate high levels of customer care.

CARING FOR CUSTOMERS DURING AN INCIDENT

Incident management provides an opportunity to demonstrate the highest levels of customer care. Research shows that customers are less concerned with the time taken to deliver a response, and more concerned with receiving reassurance that their problems are being resolved. Operations like the RAC Personal Incident Manager or disaster recovery services show that personal care can be delivered on a national scale and can embrace complex scenarios. Considerable infrastructure and communications resources are required to deliver a consistent standard of service round the clock, but the investment in this level of service can result in high levels of customer satisfaction.

USING TECHNOLOGY TO IMPROVE CUSTOMER SERVICE

Technology provides a valuable support to personal skills in delivering the highest standards of customer service. Technology can allow the centralisation of customer response through a national call reception centre and the introduction of centres of excellence, providing consistent support to customers nationwide. The implementation of a company-wide customer care training programme ensures that all staff are customer focused and balances the investment in technology. As for the previous section, considerable infrastructure and communications resources are required to deliver a consistent standard of service round the clock, but the investment in this level of service can result in high levels of customer satisfaction.

USING COMMUNICATIONS TO ENHANCE A SERVICE

First Direct have used information technology and communications in an innovative way, developing a new customer focused service that has improved customer contact, rather than reduced it. The 'direct' approach is now being used by other companies and providing them with successful, profitable business. The service provides high levels of customer convenience and allows a company to deliver consistently high standards of service to all customers, wherever they are located.

CUSTOMER CLUBS

Customer clubs are an effective form of relationship marketing that enable a company to add value to their customer services and differentiate a service. Clubs can be targeted at specific sectors of the market and offer valuable opportunities to achieve higher levels of customer contact and stronger business relationships. In business markets, clubs should offer customers tangible business benefits and help to achieve high levels of customer retention. Clubs must be active and companies should ensure that customers receive a constant stream of offers to maintain interest.

HELPING CUSTOMERS IMPROVE THEIR BUSINESS PERFORMANCE

Manufacturers and distributors are improving their own market penetration by working closely with customers to help them improve their own business performance. The support can take a number of different forms, including business support, training, marketing support, joint ventures or improved delivery service and pricing. By focusing on the customer's business requirements, the manufacturer can develop a tailored service that builds effective working relationships and increases account control.

HELPING YOUR CUSTOMERS MAKE BUSINESS DECISIONS

This chapter explains how you can use high-level management briefings to improve relationships with your customers and position your company as a strategic supplier. Seminars and management briefings are valuable techniques for communicating with senior executives and this form of direct contact can be supplemented by published management guides. The programme helps your customers to improve skills at a level that would not normally be available through conventional training.

MAKING IT EASIER FOR CUSTOMERS TO BUY

Making it easier for your customers to buy is a sure way of improving customer satisfaction. Electronic ordering and payments systems, for example, can reduce mountains of paperwork. Communications also make it easier for your key customers to obtain up-to-date commercial and delivery information and lay the foundation for processes such as Just-In-Time which enable you to build even stronger customer links. You can also go further and develop customised products that are unique to the customer. Providing your customers with a single point of access for all enquiries makes it easier for them to do business and allows you to control the quality of customer contact. Customers with branches around the country or a requirement for delivering a local service to their own customers can take advantage of your local networks.

REWARDING LOYAL CUSTOMERS

Customer loyalty programmes provide a basis for demonstrating high levels of customer care and differentiating the level of service. It is important that the reward reflects the company's customer service values and increases customer satisfaction. Although incentive programmes are used as part of a sales promotion programme, they also have a strategic role in building effective customer relationships. The most effective customer loyalty programmes not only reward regular customers, they also provide information on their purchasing patterns as a basis for future product and service development.

TOWARDS PARTNERSHIP

This chapter introduces the concept of partnership and describes why it is important for you to build relationships with your customers to secure long-term business. It explains how you can co-operate with partners to win business or utilise partnership to add value to your products or services. If you need to improve local marketing performance, partnership could help you achieve that. You can also utilise partnership to develop a joint market or spread the risk in undertaking a major project. One of the most important factors behind partnership is reducing costs. The chapter shows how you could develop partnership by building links through technology, provide a broader service, or differentiate a service. There are many important factors behind partnership including increasing competition in the market-place, higher customer expectations, pressure on costs, and rapid technological change. Partnership is also important to companies aiming to compete in wider markets, undertaking rapid new product development, or overcoming skills shortages. The introduction of new business processes such as Just-In-Time or core skills development requires partnership to succeed.

LIFE CYCLE SERVICES

The life cycle is a valuable concept for understanding a customer's business and focusing a service operation on customer's needs. Companies who are already providing customers with specific types of service, such as consultancy, can use the life cycle concept to identify other opportunities in the four stages of consult, design, implement and manage. The process ensures that customers receive the right level of support at each stage and builds long-term relationships.

OFFERING CUSTOMERS YOUR SKILLS

Services make a major contribution to account control by increasing the frequency of contact between product purchase and helping your customers improve their business performance. As well as increasing contact, they also represent an opportunity to increase revenue and profitability. To identify service opportunities, you should assess business scenarios faced by your customers – what problems can your services overcome. Many companies who provided their own support services internally are now outsourcing to reduce costs and increase flexibility, and this provides a further opportunity to build the customer's dependence on your services. Consultancy, technical support, project management, training, and maintenance services are among the most important services and they contribute in different ways to key account control and development. If you are providing a 'total solution' to your customers, you must ensure that all the services are delivered to a consistent quality standard. Alternatively, you can work with a service partner, provided the partner can meet your quality standards.

CONSISTENT SERVICE NATIONWIDE

This chapter describes one of the major problems faced by companies marketing through multiple outlets – how to ensure that customers receive the same standard of service in every branch. It shows how consistency can be used as basis for branding local outlets in the same way as products. The chapter describes how quality standards such as BS 5750 are increasingly used at local level to measure and monitor performance in line with agreed standards. Staff skills are a key element of consistent performance and the chapter shows how local skills profiles are used to develop targeted training programmes. It is essential to communicate the benefits of training to local management and staff and to offer them flexible training options. The chapter provides examples of this and shows how some organisations deal with the problem of performance scatter by concentrating resources in centres of excellence or by utilising best practice from around their networks. The second part of the chapter explains the importance of consistent visual standards, explaining the scope of corporate identity programmes and showing how they reflect changing standards of customer care.

RECOGNISING CUSTOMER SATISFACTION

This chapter shows the importance of measuring customer satisfaction through customer surveys and customer comments can be used to compile customer satisfaction guides. Finally, the chapter shows how incentive and recognition schemes can be used to motivate local staff to achieve increasingly higher standards of customer satisfaction.

MEASURING SERVICE WITH QUALITY STANDARDS

Quality techniques can be applied to the measurement and control of customer service as a means of monitoring performance and improving standards. Quality standards provide a valuable competitive differentiator and demonstrate a commitment to customer service. It is important to apply quality standards to customer-facing tasks and to involve customers in assessing performance.

2

LEADING FROM THE TOP

This chapter outlines the important management activities needed to establish and operate customer focus and provides a broad overview of a senior executive's role. The tasks include:

- making strategic decisions to commit your company to customer focus
- setting standards and introducing quality processes
- transforming the culture of the organisation
- building high level relationships with key account customers
- introducing new services and customer care activities
- demonstrating a personal commitment to customer service.

It is vital that customer focus programmes are driven from the top because, without top-level commitment, it is difficult for a manager to take the fundamental decisions that may be needed to transform the culture of an organisation. Customer focus often has 'champions' within an organisation – marketing or sales staff who can see the business benefits of improving relationships with customers, but they may not have the authority to take all the decisions that are necessary. Customer focus requires vision and strong leadership because the 'champion' is committing a company to a course of action which can impact on its prospects for many years ahead. Setting up customer focus is not like opening an account for a new customer, it means aligning your business objectives with your customers' needs and focusing on that relationship to the possible exclusion of other business opportunities. Customer focus decisions are not to be taken lightly.

TRANSFORMING THE CULTURE OF THE ORGANISATION

Sir Alastair Grant, Chairman and Chief Executive of the Argyll Group Plc shows how leadership and a striving for excellence can penetrate every corner of an organisation:

I have a dream about the future of Safeway. One day we shall have 500 stores, each perfectly adapted to the needs of the community it serves; we shall sell 20,000 products of which a third will be Safeway own brand; these own brands will match or beat the quality of the leading proprietary brands; we shall trade seven days a week and every minute that we are open, we shall fully satisfy every customer.

We shall be known and loved by every consumer; known and respected by every supplier; known and admired by every financial institution; known and valued by every member of government; known and understood by every journalist. We are, I judge, about 60 per cent of the way towards my dream. Our marketing reflects both where we are and where we want to be. I apply a marketing point of view to pretty well everything we do and I work at making the idea of marketing pervasive throughout the business.

This mission statement sets the direction for everyone in the business. It shows that every manager and every employee is concerned with meeting customer needs, all of the time, whatever they do – and that customers, in many ways, include suppliers, journalists, members of government as well as consumers. The customer tells us 'where we are and where we want to be'; so in managing and planning the future we must always keep the customer in mind. 'We shall have 500 stores each perfectly adapted to the needs of the community it serves'; we need to be flexible in our approach to our customers and not impose rigid policies which suit our internal requirements. 'Every minute that we are open, we shall fully satisfy every customer'; that is the ultimate challenge to every manager. It is the reason why the customer must be the focus for every manager.

The vision itself counts for nothing unless it is accompanied by action from the top. Senior executives who demonstrate a personal commitment to customer focus by setting their own personal quality standards, taking part in customer meetings and participating in improvement programmes set an example for everyone in the organisation. By adopting a high profile, they can attract media attention and build awareness of the company's capability and commitment.

Customer focus depends, not just on the actions of a few individuals, but on the total commitment of everyone in the organisation. In a manufacturing company, for example, some of the critical processes are carried out by people who do not see their jobs as customer focused – invoice clerks, delivery drivers, maintenance engineers, telephone receptionists, warehouse staff and development engineers. However, their role is crucial to efficient day-to-day customer service and without their commitment and understanding, a drive for total customer focus is likely to fail. There are a number of important tasks:

- provide a vision of the way your company should operate and how your customers should see the company
- communicate the practical implications of customer focus to everyone in

your organisation
- present the vision in terms of tangible objectives for each department within the organisation
- formulate an action plan that will enable each department to achieve their objectives
- allocate the resources to achieve departmental objectives
- introduce a reporting mechanism that will enable the departments to communicate with each other and demonstrate overall corporate progress
- allocate resources to motivation and incentive programmes designed to improve organisational performance
- develop recognition schemes to reward improvement.

TAKING PERSONAL ACCOUNTABILITY

As well as providing the vision, leaders also have to be accountable for the quality of customer service. Dell Computers appointed Billy Martin as European Customer Service Director with overall responsibility for service excellence. This is important when customer service is traditionally seen as a specific departmental responsibility. Dell had grown rapidly by establishing a reputation for selling quality personal computers at competitive prices direct to users and backing that with a highly effective support programme that included unlimited telephone support. However, they realised that their initial success, with sales growth of around 100 per cent a year, was being threatened by competitors who were copying their approach to customer service.

Dell identified four key responsibilities for their customer service director:

- improving the performance of all customer focused activities, department by department, to make each one as efficient as possible
- establishing customer focus standards based on customer needs and industry best practice. Dell identified service-led organisations such as American Airlines and Federal Express as important benchmarks for customer focused companies
- monitoring quality processes to ensure that they reflect customer needs. Other departments have functional responsibility for quality, but the customer service director measures the 'quality of quality'
- ensuring customer feedback. Dell's direct sales operations and telephone support depend on effective telephone performance, so the customer service director ensures that customers are regularly called back to check whether they were satisfied with the service and to deal with any problems.

ASSESSING THE RISK

Although customer focus offers many business benefits, it also offers a high level of risk. Your senior management team should be closely involved in the decision-making process and should include executives responsible for finance, corporate planning, human resources and production. In a smaller organisation, these functions may be combined, but it is essential that the strategic customer focus decisions are made by the people who run the company.

Recruitment consultants MSL, who have a firsthand view of executive recruitment policies in the field of customer service, commented that there was still a clear split in company attitudes. As businesses responded to competitive pressures, increasing numbers were considering high-level customer service appointments, but many companies were simply bolting the process on to traditional functions such as marketing, distribution, production and product development, where the responsible executive had either an administrative or an operational role.

The following are some of the factors your executive team should use to analyse the potential benefits of customer focus and, conversely, the risks of not developing it:

- Are your competitors likely to gain ground by building closer relationships with customers?
- If your competitors' future plans include levels of customer service which your company is currently unable to match, are you likely to lose future growth opportunities?
- If your competitors dominate a market sector through quality customer service, are you likely to lose access to that market? What sort of risk does that pose?
- If your business-to-business customers are determined to work only with customer focused companies and reduce the number of suppliers, do you run the risk of being excluded from some of the most important markets?

These are the risks you must assess if you do not pursue customer focus policies, or if you do not meet the standards set by a dominant competitor. Such risks must be weighed carefully against the potential gains of customer focus, and then reviewed again to assess the risks in meeting the requirements of establishing the right levels of customer service. Customer focus will change your organisation and you need to be certain that you can meet the challenges and the costs of change. These are some of the fundamental questions you should ask:

- What changes will be required to meet the short- and long-term requirements of customer focus?

- How will customers react?
- Do the customer focus benefits outweigh any potential loss of business from customers who might defect to competitors?
- Are your quality processes sufficient to meet your customer focus requirements?
- What would be the cost and implications of upgrading those quality standards?
- Are current skills and staffing levels sufficient to meet the potential demands of customer focus?
- What would be the cost of recruiting and developing new skills?
- Do you have the management skills to meet the changing requirements of customer focus?
- Could your current management team grow into their new role through training and personal development, or would you have to recruit and build a new management team?
- What are the financial implications of customer focus in terms of additional working capital or new investment to increase levels of service or improve quality?
- Given that the development of customer focus will take up a great deal of senior management time and effort, can you commit your executive team, or will it divert them from other strategically important tasks?

There are likely to be many other factors specific to your industry or specific to a particular group of customers which must be considered, but these are questions that every company must consider because they impact on both day-to-day activities and the long-term development of the business. After assessing the different types of risk described in this chapter, ask your executive team to consider two other important questions:

- Is the level of change and the anticipated cost in line with your strategic plans?
- Is a change in your strategic direction likely to have a greater or lesser benefit to your long-term business prospects?

Before committing your organisation to customer focus, you must be sure that you have made the right decision. A programme that benefits your customers but locks you into a cycle of increased costs and distracts you from your long-term goals is a one-way process and may not be in your best interests.

COMMITTING RESOURCES TO PARTNERSHIP

If you decide that the benefits of customer focus outweigh the risks, you must commit your whole organisation. As subsequent chapters show, this means committing time to set up and manage a customer focused organisation, committing people and developing their skills and committing funds to investing in new levels of service. This commitment does not suddenly begin when customer focus starts to operate, there is a considerable commitment in planning customer focus and deciding how it will operate. In addition, you and your senior executive team must decide whether you will be involved throughout the process or whether you will delegate tasks to other members of staff and you must determine the level of resources you will commit to each stage.

COMMITTING YOUR ORGANISATION TO CUSTOMER FOCUS

In this phase, you will be changing attitudes within the organisation, developing skills and establishing the processes that will be needed for customer focus. The important actions are discussed in more detail later in this chapter, but you will have to commit time and resources in a number of different areas:

- setting the overall direction for change and providing a corporate plan
- developing a mission statement and achieving the commitment of all staff to the mission
- developing the guidelines for an internal communications programme and allocating funds to the programme
- establishing the skills requirements and allocating a budget for recruitment and training
- introducing appropriate quality standards and allocating funds to quality training and the introduction of essential quality processes
- selecting and appointing the team which will drive the programme forward and allocating funds to the key tasks they identify.

This first stage will get your organisation into shape. It will involve a considerable amount of your time in setting the overall direction and managing progress, but this involvement will reduce as customer focus becomes the company norm. Allocating the right level of funds at this stage means that you can deal with the changing requirements of customer focus from day one.

INTRODUCING CUSTOMER FOCUS

An effective leader sets the customer focus standards for the whole organisation. Peter Bonfield, Chairman of ICL, took personal responsibility for turning the company into a quality organisation and set his own personal customer focus standards. His high personal profile ensured that no one could fail to be aware of quality and customer service. Peter Bonfield played a personal role in launching 'The ICL Way' to employees and to customers, explaining how quality would be central to everything the company did. As well as attending management and staff briefing meetings, Peter Bonfield maintained regular contact with press and television, taking every opportunity to explain the company's position.

This stage involves a major investment in internal communications at many different levels within the organisation. Your key tasks at this stage are to change attitudes within the organisation, and to achieve that you will have to commit people and support them with communications budgets. The important tasks would include:

● briefing other senior executives on strategic direction
● holding management briefings and appointing members of the customer focus team to participate in these events
● appointing members of the customer focus team to hold detailed briefings with staff groups
● developing a communications strategy and allocating funds to the operation of the communications programme.

Many of the tasks in this phase will involve the work of specialists within the customer focus team. Your role will be to set the overall direction, maintain the impetus of the programme and build effective relations with your staff and the management team.

SETTING STANDARDS

A key element in the development of customer focus is setting or meeting performance standards to ensure that customers enjoy the highest standards of service. Standards for individual departments will be the responsibility of individual managers, but the overall commitment to quality is driven by the senior executive team.

The standards can be set by research into your customers's needs or established by independent standards authorities such as the British Standards Institute. Conformance to independent standards demonstrates that you are committed to quality and prepared to subject your organisation to external assessment. The subject of quality management is outside the scope of this book, but quality depends on effective leadership and a strong sense of direction from the executive team. The key management tasks are to:

- demonstrate commitment to total quality within your organisation
- identify the areas and activities where independent quality measurements should be applied
- establish priorities for introducing quality processes
- appoint a quality team with responsibility for establishing quality processes and liaising with your partners' quality representatives
- allocate funds to the introduction of quality processes and the development of quality training programmes
- introduce and monitor feedback mechanisms to measure levels of customer satisfaction
- allocate funds to improvement programmes designed to increase levels of customer satisfaction.

BUILDING CUSTOMER RELATIONSHIPS

An increasing number of senior executives are taking a leading role in the development of customer relationships. Tom Farmer, Managing Director of automotive parts specialist Qwikfit, has built an excellent reputation for his company by personally contacting customers to ask about standards of service. He sets aside several evenings a week to call customers who have recently used a Qwikfit centre. It creates a positive feeling with customers to know that the managing director takes a personal interest in their views and it also helps to focus staff in the branches on customer service because they know that the managing director will be aware of any problems.

While this level of personal involvement with the customer may be unusual in consumer markets, it is essential in business-to-business markets. To ensure the success of customer focus initiatives, your team should be developing relationships at different levels within the customer organisation and you need to build a matching top-level relationship with your customer's senior executive team.

Earlier in this chapter, we reviewed the risks that you need to evaluate before committing your organisation to customer focus programmes. If you are building close working relationships with your business customers, your potential partners face similar decisions and they need your reassurance on certain key issues before they get deeply involved with you. Although it is your sales team who will make the initial contact, they may not have the experience or the authority to discuss strategic business issues with a senior management team.

By getting involved with your customer's senior executive team, you show that their business is important to your company and that you are prepared to put the full weight of your position behind the success of the relationship. Chapter 18, 'Helping your customers make business decisions', explains the importance of seminars and management briefings in helping senior executives to understand the benefits and implications of close working relationships for their organisation. By participating in this type of event, you are showing that customer focus is a strategic issue that should be discussed at board level. You will also have the opportunity to provide a firsthand account of how you would deal with the executive team's concerns. Among the questions in the minds of your customer's executive team will be:

- Does your organisation have the capability to deliver a sustained quality of service over the long term?
- Does your organisation have the resources to grow in line with changing business requirements?
- Is your organisation flexible enough to respond to changing business and market requirements?
- How important is customer focus to your organisation and how would you demonstrate your commitment to success?
- Will your customers have access to your senior management team and what escalation procedures will be in place in the event of any problem?

By helping senior executives to make decisions about customer focused business relationships, you can ensure that negotiations are conducted at the right level and that your proposals will be properly evaluated.

INTRODUCING NEW CUSTOMER SERVICE INITIATIVES

As part of the development of customer focus, you may need to introduce new service initiatives so that your service is closely aligned to the needs of your customers. New initiatives can involve high levels of risk, so it is important that any decisions are made at senior level. Questions concerning these new initiatives will include:

- Will the new services evolve from your existing range?
- What is the likely development cost?
- Will the development programme interfere with other strategically important

development projects?

- Will the new services provide you with competitive advantage in any other sectors?
- If you do not develop the new service, will your competitors have an opportunity to regain lost ground with your customers?

Effective new service development will ensure that you maintain the momentum of the customer focus initiative, but the projects need to be carefully integrated with your corporate development programme to ensure that they do not affect your progress in other areas. Key actions to ensure the success of your new service initiatives include:

- setting priorities for new initiatives
- allocating sufficient funds to new service development
- encouraging and rewarding innovation
- encouraging proactive research and development in line with your partners' objectives.

INTEGRATING SUPPLIERS INTO CUSTOMER FOCUS

The quality of service you deliver to your customers depends on the quality of service your suppliers provide. If quality is one of the reasons your customers continue to buy from you, you need to be certain that you can deliver. If you are not able to deliver a complete solution within your own resources, you could work with third parties so that your staff can concentrate on their core business activities.

Working with third parties means that you are building a form of partnership with your own suppliers, so you need to assess the potential of that relationship in the same way as your customers might assess you. It is important that your senior management team develops a relationship that enables you to manage the supply chain throughout. These are the key issues you should consider:

- Can third parties carry out specific activities more cost effectively than your staff?
- Can they carry out the activities to the same quality standards?
- Can you integrate their quality systems with yours?
- Would a strategic alliance with a third party provide you with a more effective solution to your customers' needs?
- Will third parties provide you with access to scarce technology or specialist skills so that you can deliver a higher standard of service?

- Could you develop the same skills or resources within your own organisation?
- What benefits do you offer the third parties and how dependent are they on you?

By selecting third party suppliers carefully and developing effective relationships, you can improve the performance of your own organisation and provide an extremely high standard of service to your customers. It is important that these issues are discussed at a senior level.

MONITORING CUSTOMER FOCUS

Day-to-day customer focused tasks will be managed at departmental and functional level. However, the involvement of the senior executive team is still important to ensure that the organisation continues to deliver the highest standards of service and to put into action any changes that are needed to meet changing customer requirements. Key senior management tasks at this stage include:

- holding regular review meetings with your staff and management team to ensure that the customer focus programme continues to meet its objectives
- monitoring the performance of your organisation and assessing any feedback from your customers to see whether you need to initiate further changes
- reviewing new investment requirements and allocating funding
- holding regular reviews of the benefits and impact of customer focus to see whether you need to change your overall policy
- assessing opportunities to develop closer relationships with your customers
- allocating resources to managing and supporting the efficient operation of customer focus activities.

SUMMARY

This chapter has looked at the role of the senior executive and examined the key management actions needed for the development of a customer focused organisation. It has explained how the strategic customer focus decisions need to be taken by a senior executive team and outlined the risks and opportunities that should be assessed before committing an organisation to customer focus. It has shown that there may be risks in not pursuing a customer focused strategy, allowing competitors to gain ground, but there are equal risks in pursuing a form of customer focus that puts considerable strain on an organisation's resources. The resource requirements change at each stage of customer focus and senior executives need to develop a policy for developing the right customer focus team.

Issues such as skills development and investment need to be carefully considered. Executives must also set easily measured standards that enable performance to be monitored and ensure the highest standards of quality. To achieve new standards, it may be necessary to transform the culture of an organisation; this requires vision and strong leadership, and senior executives will play a vital role. It is also important for senior executives to build good working relationships with their counterparts in customer organisations because this demonstrates serious commitment to customer focus.

New service development may be an important element in a customer focus strategy, and senior executives must review the risks and implications. Decisions must also be taken about the benefits and risks of working with third parties. Third parties may fill gaps in a company's own resources, but they should only be used if they can provide a quality service that will contribute to overall customer satisfaction.

Self-assessment checklist

- Do you involve your senior management team in the assessment of customer focus opportunities and risks?

- What opportunities does customer focus offer you?

- What are the risks in pursuing a customer focused strategy?

- Have you identified the resources required at each stage of the customer focus programme?

- Can you delegate some of the customer focus tasks?

- What will your involvement be at each stage?

- Are you involved in high-level contact with your customers?

- Have you established procedures for monitoring your organisation's customer service performance?

- Does your organisation have recognised quality standards?

- Are those standards measured to relevant independent standards?

- Can you measure your partners' satisfaction with your performance against standards?

- Do you need to change the culture of your organisation to achieve customer focus standards?

- Do you have a corporate vision and do staff understand it?

- Do you demonstrate personal commitment to customer service?

- Can you identify opportunities to make direct contact with customers on a regular basis?

- How important are high-level relationships to the success of a customer focus programme?

- Do you and your senior executive team participate in high-level relationships?

- Can you identify opportunities for improving high-level relationships?

- Are you confident that your customers' executive team has all the information it needs to make decisions about your commitment to their business?

- How important are new service initiatives to the success of partnership?

- Have you evaluated the risks in pursuing a new service development programme?

- Do you have the resources to pursue a separate programme?

- How important are third parties to the success of your customer focus programme?

- Can you identify suppliers who might work in partnership with you to improve the overall performance of the supply chain?

- Can you use third parties to supplement your own resources and deliver higher standards of service?

3

BUILDING CUSTOMER TEAMS

This chapter looks at the importance of building the right customer service team – the group of key staff who will deliver the highest standards of service to the customer and build effective long-term relationships. Effective teams are essential, not just within your own organisation, but also within your suppliers and subcontractors – by providing you with a quality service, they can help to improve the quality of the entire supply chain. Your retailers and distributors can also help you to build effective relationships with key customers by providing some of the supply and contact functions.

There are a number of important actions to achieve the highest standards of customer service team performance:

- selecting the right team to meet customers' needs
- raising awareness of customer focus
- building commitment
- developing customer focus
- operating customer care training
- establishing quality standards
- setting up internal processes to improve customer response
- supporting the customer service team
- ensuring effective communications within the team
- operating motivation and incentive programmes
- building partnership with retailers and distributors
- building relationships with suppliers and subcontractors.

SELECTING THE RIGHT TEAM

Customer focus is based on the relationships between suppliers and customers and should involve everyone in the organisation. In traditional buyer and seller scenarios, the relationship is driven by the salesforce with the occasional involvement of the technical department, but the success of total quality, customer satisfaction programmes and other customer care initiatives has demonstrated how the performance of many other staff impacts on the customer's perception of a company. Customer focus depends on a consistently high standard of customer service over a long period of time and that means building and maintaining a commitment to quality.

Depending on the size of your organisation, a customer focus team might include all of your staff or it may be a project team, representing the departments or functions that impact directly on the customer. In a large manufacturing organisation, for example, the team might include people from the following departments:

- sales
- distribution
- manufacturing
- design/development
- marketing
- communications
- personnel
- training
- purchasing
- customer service
- quality
- administration.

Although this group may not be actively involved in a team that is deciding policy, it is essential that they understand the importance of customer focus and their role in delivering the right standard of service. Within that broad group of people who affect the success of customer focus, there are likely to be smaller groups who can help to drive a customer service initiative forward. There are a number of factors which can be used to assess who should be included in the 'main team':

- Their performance directly impacts on customer satisfaction.
- They are responsible for managing change which will influence the direction of customer service.
- They will be working closely with customers.
- They will be providing services which support customers;

The 'main team' will be working to achieve customer focus objectives and will be able to draw on the skills of other 'outer team' members to provide specialist support. Some examples show how this might work in practice.

Components supplier

Johnson Controls is an American manufacturer of seats and other components for the automotive industry, with subsidiaries in Europe and other parts of the world. The company sees customer focus as key to its long-term success and cultivates the team ethic as a major element of corporate strategy. When the company set up a new manufacturing plant in Spain to provide a local service to domestic car plants, it brought in a project team from other European subsidiaries. The project team was able to bring together the right skills plus an understanding of customer needs in the European market. The result was a factory that represented best practice and reflected customer needs.

An increasing number of components suppliers work in partnership with their customers to provide important business benefits, including guaranteed levels of quality supply, and to offer the manufacturer access to specialist technology. The partnership team might include:

- the managing director, responsible for the overall direction and quality of the partnership, plus high level relationships
- the sales and marketing director, responsible for commercial policies and service development
- the production director, responsible for maintaining the overall quality of supply
- the quality manager, responsible for specific quality initiatives to meet the requirements of the partnership
- the account manager or sales representative, responsible for managing the day-to-day relationships between the supplier and the partners
- the administration manager, responsible for developing communications and systems to support the partnership
- the research and development manager, responsible for developing new products to meet partners' requirements
- the technical director, responsible for providing technical support to partners and managing technical relationships between the parties.

This team would be actively involved in maintaining relationships with the partner and would support the functions that are vital to the success of the partnership.

Capital equipment manufacturer

When computer manufacturer, ICL, wanted to build closer working relationships with key account customers, it produced a care and support manual which explained the benefits of partnership. The manual outlined how ICL delivered customer service and described the actions the company had taken to improve customer service standards. The manual also included a guide to the key staff in ICL and the customer company who would be working together. This personnel guide not only helped customer and supplier to understand each other's business, it demonstrated how ICL used a team approach to deliver the highest standards of customer satisfaction.

Capital equipment manufacturers provide their customers with a high level of technical co-operation and support to ensure that the customer is able to get an effective return on the investment and obtain a high level of business benefits in the shortest possible time. Introducing the new equipment means considerable organisational change and skills development so the initial emphasis within the customer team will be on customer support through the implementation period. The team will include staff who can help the customer to manage the process of change, but the emphasis will be on customer support throughout the implementation period.

The team might include:

- the managing director, to ensure effective high level relationships;
- the sales and marketing director, responsible for the detailed commercial negotiations
- the customer service director, responsible for developing the right support programme to ensure effective implementation
- the training manager, to help the customer develop the skills to take advantage of the new products
- project managers, responsible for implementing the new system
- the technical support manager, responsible for providing ongoing advice and support to the customer's team during the start-up period.

The composition of this team is weighted towards achieving a rapid, successful implementation of complex capital equipment. After the installation, the emphasis within the team will change to helping the customer make the most of the investment. Other team members will now become more important, including:

- applications engineers, to help the customer's team fine tune or adapt the equipment to new tasks
- business development managers, to help the customer's team make the most effective business use of the investment
- support managers, to ensure that the customer enjoys high standards of service.

This change in team membership is an important consideration. Customer focus is not a static activity. It evolves and the team should evolve to meet your customer's changing requirements.

Professional consultancy

A professional consultancy such as a marketing services company is delivering a service which supports customers' business objectives and the team will be focused on the delivery of the service. Logistics, supply and other support services are less important. In a small consultancy, personal service is very important and the team will include those people who are directly involved with the partner's business. The team might include:

- the senior partner, responsible for the overall direction of the business
- the principle marketing consultant, responsible for the quality of the service
- the marketing consultants who handle clients' business on a day-to-day basis
- specialist consultants in disciplines such as research and communications.

This team concentrates on maintaining a high standard of professional service to the client and integrates its services so that the client gets comprehensive professional advice. In the management consultancy business, there is an increasing overlap between strategic consultancy and information systems consultancy. Andersen Consulting has developed skills within the practice to deliver both strategic and information systems consultancy, and also works closely with information systems partners to ensure that the client gets the best advice from a strategic and practical point of view.

Service organisation

A company that provides services such as repair and maintenance needs to build a team that combines the right skills with an infrastructure that makes it easy for the customer to do business. The team might include:

- the managing director, responsible for the overall direction of the business;
- the operations director, responsible for developing an infrastructure that meets the partner's business requirements
- the service director, responsible for the delivery of service
- the service development director, responsible for introducing new services
- senior managers, responsible for specific service activities
- branch managers, responsible for the quality of local service delivery
- service receptionists who deal with customers with service queries
- service technicians who deliver the service
- support staff who provide backup services to the technicians.

These examples of customer focus teams show that the company must be completely focused on your customers' business and it must include senior executives who are driving the project from the top, as well as the staff whose actions directly influence the success of the customer relationship.

RAISING AWARENESS OF CUSTOMER FOCUS

The members of a customer focus team will be directly involved with customers and they will drive the programme forward. In a number of organisations, they are known as 'champions', and they have a responsibility for motivating other members of staff who influence success. In practice, customer focus will always be the responsibility of a small group of people like this but it is important to involve everyone in the organisation. This proceeds through a number of stages:

- auditing current awareness of customer service
- identifying the most important contacts and influencers within the organisation
- raising levels of awareness through planned internal communications
- monitoring levels of awareness.

When ICL wanted to build partnership through their customer service activities, they knew that they would have to change attitudes within their own organisation as well as within their customer base. The customer service division had been used to delivering maintenance services, but they would now be responsible for delivering a wider range of professional services, and their role would be crucial in building the success of the partnership. ICL realised that success would depend on understanding and commitment throughout the division and they knew that they would have to undertake a major training programme to develop the new skills needed to deliver an entirely different service.

After making the preliminary structural changes and setting up training programmes, they carried out an audit of the key people within the division to assess the level of understanding of the direction they were taking. The audit included:

- questionnaires to all members of staff
- interviews with selected staff
- an evaluation of the messages in internal communications media.

The audit revealed that a significant proportion of the staff were not aware of the full implications of the changes that were taking place and this could have had an adverse effect on the prospects for partnership. ICL developed a communications programme to increase levels of awareness of their new direction. The communications programme covered a wide variety of media including videos, presentations, recruitment advertisements, induction brochures, staff magazines, training communications and team briefing material. Communications staff planned each publication and presentation carefully to ensure that it included 'positioning messages' which built a perception of a dynamic professional services organisation that was important to the future success of the company. Key messages included:

- Services make an important contribution to revenue and profit.
- Services build long-term partnership with clients.
- The introduction of new professional services would help ICL become a strategic supplier, vital to the client's business success.
- Total quality was essential to the success of the operation.
- Everyone in the division contributed to the success of partnership.

This programme of planned communications ensured that messages about the changing role of the division were communicated consistently, and this helped to raise awareness.

BUILDING COMMITMENT TO CUSTOMER FOCUS

Just raising awareness may not be enough to push customer focus forward. You may have to operate a higher profile campaign and encourage staff. By explaining how customer focus impacts on the success of the business and on their own personal prospects, you can encourage your staff to take specific action.

Ford Motor Company wanted to improve the commitment of staff who maintained day-to-day contact with distributors – an essential element in achieving high levels of customer service. Because of pressure of work and an increasing number of incoming calls, the staff had been forced to take longer to answer calls and deal with enquiries. Improvement was vital, so Ford developed a high profile campaign which built team spirit and introduced an element of competition into departmental activities.

The campaign was based on the television programme 'MASH' – in this case an acronym for 'Make Active Service Happen'. Customer response teams were divided into 'platoons' who were given awards for achievement in battle, i.e. answering calls or responding to enquiries within a specified time. There were additional bonus points for exceptional performance – heroic deeds – and deductions for slips or poor performance – the walking wounded. The points were clearly displayed throughout the department and updated on a daily basis so that attention was constantly focused on performance. The results were linked to a long-term incentive programme and there were a number of 'spot prizes' to encourage continued effort. The campaign included an element of fun as well as effort and gained additional interest through activities and promotional items on a related military theme. For example, to launch the programme, uniformed soldiers raided the department on day one and set up some of the campaign material in front of the staff. An open day featuring combat games and other military themes helped to maintain interest during the event.

Although the 'MASH' theme helped to add an element of fun and interest to the campaign, the purpose of the campaign was serious – to achieve the total involvement and commitment of the staff in an activity that was critical to the successful relationships with distributors.

DEVELOPING CUSTOMER FOCUS IN THE TEAM

As part of the drive for customer satisfaction, it is important to focus the attention of the entire organisation on the customer so that staff can understand the needs of customers and understand why customer care is so important. Companies who market their products through retail outlets develop customer focus standards which are essential to maintain the highest standards of customer service. Customer focus standards are based on research into customer attitudes and feedback from customer satisfaction surveys.

These customer focus standards reflect the factors that customers have indicated are most important and they help an organisation to improve their competitive performance and achieve high levels of customer satisfaction. Chapter 7, 'Improving convenience for customers', describes how the Post Office took the opportunity to improve customer service when it relocated some of its offices away from traditional high street locations.

For a retail outlet, customer focus standards might include the following elements:

- convenience of location
- opening hours
- easy access and parking
- speed of service or reception
- choice
- helpful staff
- product knowledge.

In developing their action plans, retailers know that they must concentrate their efforts on achieving the highest standards in these areas. The same principles can be applied to partnership situations. By identifying the factors that are critical to the success of the partnership, it is possible to establish standards that everyone in the organisation must adhere to. These standards would form the basis of training and action programmes to improve standards and would be used as the focal point of motivation and incentive programmes.

Another approach to developing customer focus is to 'put yourself in your customers' shoes'. Here, verbatim comments on research results are used to demonstrate customer attitudes to different standards of service. Many surveys and questionnaires incorporate sections which allow customers to explain 'in their own words' how they feel about a product or service and invite them to comment in detail on a specific problem. Car manufacturers, for example, issue customer satisfaction questionnaires which cover customers' attitudes to different departments within a dealership. Verbatim comments are used in dealership guides to improving customer satisfaction and issued to all departments within a dealership to show how departmental standards impact on customer satisfaction.

Technicians, for example, felt that they were not responsible for customer care, but comments like these can soon change their views: 'As soon as I left the service station, I realised that the fault had not been rectified'; 'I found it irritating that I had to clean out the ashtray – I'm a non-smoker'; 'there were grease marks all over the seat and steering wheel – it could have ruined my clothes'. These comments make technicians realise that there is more to their jobs than just completing the job on time. They must ensure that they pay attention to factors such as quality of work, cleanliness and consideration for the customer. Car manufacturers know that if all departments in a dealership achieve high levels of customer focus, there is a good chance that the customer will be satisfied and will return to the dealership for further work and, eventually, for a new car. They are developing customer focus to ensure customer loyalty and, in a partnership environment, that attitude is vital to the continued success of the partnership.

To ensure that you have the right level of customer focus in your organisation:

- identify the departments and individual staff whose contribution has a direct impact on customer satisfaction
- assess the key elements of customer satisfaction from your customers' point of view
- research current levels of customer satisfaction or ask for comments on your performance in critical areas
- make sure that everyone in the organisation – managers and staff – is aware of customers' expectations and current perception of their performance
- introduce improvement programmes in potential problem areas.

Customer focus standards are covered in more detail in Chapters 4, 5 and 6.

TRAINING IN CUSTOMER CARE

Customer focus standards help staff understand their role in building customer satisfaction. They can also form the basis of customer care training programmes. Customer care training concentrates on building personal skills and understanding of the customer's needs and, in theory, every member of your staff should participate in the programme. However, given the time and resources available, it may be more important to set priorities and introduce customer care training gradually – beginning with the people whose actions directly affect the success of the customer focus programme. Potential trainees would include:

- the customer focus team
- staff who are in direct contact with customers
- staff who provide essential support services
- managers of the staff who deliver customer care.

Training can be delivered in a number of ways:

- using the resources of a specialist customer care training consultancy to deliver tailored training programmes
- using your own training resources to deliver tailored programmes
- sending staff to standard external customer care training courses
- using customer care videos or other training materials to provide a basic training in customer care
- appointing a customer care specialist with responsibility for developing staff skills
- issuing printed guides to customer care, explaining the importance of the right attitude and the actions that should be taken to deliver high standards.

Improving customer care requires a number of different management actions:

- selecting a training programme that is appropriate to your organisation
- providing essential support processes to the staff who deliver customer care
- rewarding achievement.

Any imbalance in the customer care programme will put the partnership at risk. Commentators on customer care point out that there are two aspects – material service and personal service. Material service is the system or the technology which enables an organisation to deliver customer care – an efficient telephone system, on-line ordering, Just-In-Time delivery systems. These are the customer response processes described later in this chapter and it is essential that they are managed efficiently to improve service to customers. However, unless they are accompanied by the right level of personal service, the investment in material service will be wasted. Telephones that are not answered within a certain time, slow response to enquiries, or a poor response to a customer query can have a damaging effect on customer relations. The training programme must therefore ensure that staff understand the support processes and programmes available to them, and have the attitude to make the most effective use of them.

One of the most successful and widely recognised customer care training programmes was undertaken by British Airways during the 1980s. In 1982, the decision was taken to privatise the airline. External competitive pressures required an internal transformation from a 'bureaucratic and militaristic' organisation to a 'service-oriented and market-driven' one. The five-year transformation saw successful privatisation, an increase in cargo and passenger revenue, and an increase in share price.

Among the key activities were:

- setting up comprehensive training programmes
- modifying the structure, individual's jobs and work procedures
- conducting a company-wide survey to assess organisational culture and using data to pinpoint required changes
- collecting information from staff on what they felt needed to be changed and responding to those views.

Achieving the right level of customer care involved three stages:

- making people aware of the need for change, helping them understand their role, making them receptive to change
- making the actual changes to cause people to behave differently, making changes in organisation structure, enabling different interpersonal relationships
- stabilising these changes by institutionalising them, e.g. with new reward or recruitment systems.

This programme lasted some three and a half years and covered more than 20,000 people in customer care positions. A project on this scale shows that the development of customer care is not a minor undertaking – it is a long-term company-wide process which involves staff at every level. The programme was so successful that British Airways set up a separate training division – Speedwing Training – to offer customer service training to their business partners, including travel agents, and to other organisations who needed to deliver high levels of customer care to obtain a competitive edge.

IMPROVING INTERNAL PROCESSES

The last section outlined some of the processes that can be used to deliver high standards of customer care – the material service. By providing a high level of automation and support, you can free staff to concentrate on personal service and reduce the risk of inconsistent service delivery. When ICL introduced a new customer service strategy to strengthen partnership with key customers, they developed a series of support processes to ensure that staff could provide customers with a rapid quality response. The main elements of the strategy were:

- the Connection – a single service reception centre
- centres of excellence
- service tools.

The Connection was a single access point for all customer queries. Customers could report faults or problems, book service calls, obtain information on products or services, query progress on problem resolution or obtain advice and guidance on related queries within their own organisation. The reception staff working in the Connection take details of the call and contact the appropriate specialist who then calls the customer back within an agreed time-scale. The staff also monitor the progress of the response to queries and provide an escalation procedure for queries that cannot be resolved within agreed times. The entire process of call reception and response is monitored to BS 5750 quality standards so that customers can feel confident that their queries will be handled efficiently.

To ensure that staff could deliver a consistent standard of service throughout the country, ICL decided to concentrate their resources in centres of excellence. Previously, each branch had delivered service using local resources, but customers served by smaller or more remote branches were receiving poorer service. This inconsistency was not conducive to partnership, so ICL decided to utilise the communications facilities available through the Connection to deliver high standards of customer service. The staff in the Connection routed the enquiry to the appropriate centre of excellence and suitable resources were allocated. This allowed ICL to develop its own skills in a planned way and to allocate resources to meet customers' requirements rather than geographical necessity.

CUSTOMER FOCUS IN THE SALESFORCE

The role of the salesforce changes in a customer focused environment. Instead of concentrating on short-term sales and new business development, the salesforce are now responsible for developing effective long-term relationships with customers. To use an analogy, they become farmers rather than hunters, and much of their time will be spent co-ordinating the activities of other members of staff. Support services, therefore become important to ensure that the salesforce can call on a wide range of skills to meet customers' changing requirements. The salesforce will be working closely with the following groups of people within the customer team:

- technical staff
- production and logistics specialists
- administration staff
- sales administration staff
- customer service staff.

The other important change for the salesforce is that they are likely to be selling services, as well as products. In the traditional sales environment, they would have been given a remuneration package based on achievement of specific sales targets; they will now be responsible for selling services that are of comparatively low value in monetary terms, but extremely valuable in building long-term customer relationships. They will also be increasing the frequency and breadth of contact – making proactive customer care calls to ensure that customers are satisfied with the standard of service, holding regular review meetings to discuss progress on projects, presenting proposals to senior members of staff, and setting up joint projects to further enhance customer relationships. These tasks require new skills that are not part of the traditional salesforce development programme and new forms of training should be introduced to cover:

- presentation techniques to ensure that the sales staff are able to present complex subjects to large groups, when most of their experience has been in one-to-one situations
- managing relationships to ensure that they understand the importance of long-term relationships and to help them identify the key personnel who should be included in the relationship
- co-ordinating teams to help them work with other members of the team by improving their communications and interpersonal skills
- project management skills to help them plan and co-ordinate large-scale, long-term projects
- customer care skills to ensure that they are aware of partners' expectations, and to help them encourage other staff to deliver the highest standards of service.

Training will ensure that the salesforce play a central role in the development of effective customer relationships and deliver a professional service.

A customer focus team works effectively when it is communicating effectively, and the salesforce can play a valuable co-ordinating role in both formal and informal communications. A planned communications programme will ensure that there are no misunderstandings or missed opportunities. Formal communications would include regular progress meetings and reporting procedures so that all members are kept up to date; informal communications thrive in an environment where small groups within the customer focus team are encouraged to take the initiative and progress small projects before involving the whole team.

MOTIVATION AND INCENTIVE PROGRAMMES

Encouraging staff to deliver the highest standards of customer service is an integral part of customer focus development, and the team should be involved in planning and operating programmes. Incentive programmes are widely used as a tool to increase short-term sales performance, but they can also be used to motivate staff to improve their overall performance or they can be structured to improve performance in specific activities such as customer care or the acquisition of new skills.

Sales incentives have traditionally been geared to moving stock quickly for tactical reasons and, as such, they are an essential sales management technique, but they can also be used in a strategic way. When a European vehicle paint manufacturer wanted to build stronger partnerships, rather than depend on a few dominant customers, they developed a year-long incentive programme for their sales development team. They wanted to encourage staff to retain business, so a structured bonus system was applied to percentage increases in business with key accounts. The company also wanted to encourage staff to acquire new skills in business development so that they could form closer working relationships with their customers at senior management level. Additional points were awarded for participation in business skills training courses and for achieving different training levels. Finally, the incentive programme awarded points for participation in a number of business development programmes which would enable staff to improve the quality of service to customers. The incentive programme encouraged overall business development rather than short-term tactical sales.

To maintain interest in the programme, the manufacturer offered different levels of prize. There were regular monthly prizes for best customer care performance with quarterly awards for best overall performance. The other value of a programme like this is that it can be used to encourage improvement using recognition and incentive programmes. By providing a quantitive basis for comparison, different departments can compete with each other to demonstrate that they offer the highest levels of satisfaction. This competitive element can be used in a number of ways:

- to stimulate departments to improve their own performance on a year-on-year basis
- to stimulate individuals to improve their own performance
- to encourage the highest standards of customer satisfaction.

The incentive programmes should be based, not just on current performance, but on improvement and it must continue to recognise improvement over a long period of time. Top-performing departments or individuals in a league receive an award or a prize. A higher status of award can be given to the individuals who achieve the very highest levels of customer satisfaction. A number of programmes operating under the banner of chairman's or president's award recognise excellence in customer satisfaction with a special award for an élite group of branches. Ford's Chairman's Award is an élite pan-European award given to the top dealers in each of 16 territories; they are taken to a top European destination where they are personally recognised by the chairman of Ford of Europe. Programmes like this help to maintain the impetus of customer care programmes; they ensure that both individuals and departments aim at continually improving standards.

BUILDING PARTNERSHIP WITH DISTRIBUTORS AND SUPPLIERS

Distributors, suppliers and other third parties can form an important element of the customer focus team. For example, if you market your products through a national or international network of distributors, you need to ensure that your customers receive a consistent standard of service from each branch in the network. The problem of 'performance scatter' can have an impact on overall customer satisfaction. Your suppliers also play a vital role in the quality of service you provide to your customers. By building effective relationships with them and aligning their quality standards with yours, you can ensure that the entire supply chain is contributing to customer satisfaction. Despite the problems of distance, the same principles of team building can be applied in this sector.

SUMMARY

This chapter has explained the importance of building effective teams within your organisation and with your suppliers and distributors. It has shown how customer focus depends on the performance of staff who are in direct contact with your customers and staff who provide essential customer support services. The members of the team vary from business to business so it is important to select a team that mirrors your customers' requirements. Many members of staff may not realise the importance of their contribution to customer satisfaction, so you need to make a positive effort to raise awareness of customer focus and build the commitment of all staff to its success. Developing customer focus standards and operating customer care training programmes help to improve staff performance in areas that are critical to success. You can also support your staff by improving or automating key customer services such as call reception, freeing staff to deliver higher standards of personal service.

The role of the salesforce will change in a customer focus environment from 'hunter to farmer'. As they are the primary link with your customers, it is essential that they are trained in new customer service skills and receive full support from the rest of the customer team. Motivation and incentive programmes can be utilised to improve the performance of the customer team, but it is essential that the programmes are structured to reflect long-term customer requirements rather than tactical sales achievements. Finally, all the steps outlined in this chapter can be applied to the development of customer focus through your suppliers and distributors. They play an important role in building complete customer satisfaction and their contribution must be encouraged.

Self-assessment checklist

- Which of your staff have a direct impact on customer satisfaction?

- Are you managing relationships at a senior level?

- What are the critical elements in the success of customer focus and who is responsible for them?

- Can you identify changing needs through the life of the customer relationship, and how will this affect the shape of the team?

- Can you assess the level of customer awareness within your organisation?

- Who needs to be aware of customer focus?

- Is your internal communications programme designed to make staff aware of the importance of customer focus?

- What are the important messages you need to communicate to your staff?

- Can you use promotional campaigns to create high levels of internal interest?

- Can you prepare a list of the important customer focus standards that influence the success of your customer relationships?

- Are staff aware of these standards?

- Do you need to develop improvement programmes to achieve higher levels of customer focus?

- Which groups of staff need customer care training?

- Do you have the resources to train all your staff in customer care or do you have to establish priorities?

- What sources of customer care training could you use?

- Are you providing 'material support' to key customer care staff?

- Can you identify areas where you can provide 'material support'?

- What forms of automation would free your staff to concentrate on customer care?

- Can you utilise 'centres of excellence' to improve the quality of customer care?

- What role does your salesforce play in developing customer relationships?

- Do they have the skills to participate fully?

- Who are the key internal contacts for the salesforce?

- What forms of support do they need to maintain effective customer relations?

- Is there an effective communications programme to support the activities of the customer team?

- Do you need to motivate your staff to achieve target levels of customer satisfaction?

- Can you adapt tactical sales incentive programmes to meet the long-term strategic needs of customer focus development?

- Are you motivating all the staff who influence the success of customer relationships?

- How important are suppliers and distributors to overall customer satisfaction?

- How much control and influence can you exert over distributor and supplier policy?

- Can you maintain consistent standards of performance throughout a distributor network?

4

CUSTOMER RESEARCH

This chapter explains how you can use information found within your organisation to research customer needs and how you can use the information to assess the likely success of customer focus. The chapter covers a number of different stages in the process:

- analysing customer information
- researching customer requirements
- assessing competitive threats
- analysing customer attitudes to your business
- analysing customer markets
- understanding customer strategies
- assessing your value to your customers' business.

By conducting a thorough analysis of your customers' business operations, you can relate your plans to their business plans to see whether there is a viable long-term partnership opportunity.

CUSTOMER INFORMATION

Customer focus opportunities can be driven by the supplier or by the customer. Information is readily available in your own customer records that can help you to take the leading role and present your customers with the highest standards of service. What, for example, do your customers' corporate brochures or annual reports tell you about them? Other questions that can be answered include:

- What are their major markets?
- What are their most important products?
- What new products have they introduced in the last year?
- What are their plans for growth?
- What problems have they identified in their market-place?
- What are the success factors in their market?

- Who are their main competitors?

You can get similar information from other sources:

- Ask your salesforce to provide a profile of your most important customers, using the above questions.
- Maintain a file of press cuttings on your customers' activities using their trade publications as a source.
- Build a file of corporate and product literature on your customers' competitors and look for press information on their market.

This information helps to build a profile of the direction your customers' business is taking. It would be used by the marketing department to shape future sales and marketing policy, but it also has a far more important role which may be overlooked – it should prompt you to ask, 'How could customer focus activities help this customer overcome problems, realise opportunities or meet objectives? How could that strengthen our position and make us an important supplier?'

Your customers may not be aware of the concept or benefits of working closely with a customer focused organisation, so the onus may be on you to take a proactive role and suggest it to them. The remainder of this chapter looks at some of the questions in more detail:

- Which customers have the greatest potential?
- How can your technical expertise or your distributor network be used as the basis of support?
- Where should you strengthen customer focus to protect your own position against competitors?

There is no single answer to the question, 'What is the value of customer focus?' You must continually analyse your customers' activities by analysing your own records or by commissioning research that highlights opportunities.

VALUE OF KEY CUSTOMERS

Although customer focus should be an overall corporate objective, the greatest potential return from customer focused activities is likely to come from your largest and most important customers and your research efforts must be focused on this group. Marketing textbooks suggest that there is a recurring pattern in the customer profiles of small and large organisations. It is based on Pareto analysis and suggests that around 80 per cent of turnover comes from 20 per cent of customers. In other words, all businesses have a small number of large customers whose purchases shape their own prospects. Although size alone is not a criteria for partnership, it makes commercial sense to protect your customer base by building stronger relationships with those key customers. Customer focus makes an important contribution.

The first stage is to analyse your customer records:

- Who are your largest customers?
- What percentage of your business do they represent?
- How dependent are you on their business continuing at the same level or growing?
- Which of the large customers has the strongest growth prospects?
- Is there a risk that any of the customers might defect to competitors?
- How long have they been doing business with you?
- How strong is the relationship with key decision makers?
- How have levels of business changed over the past three years?
- Are there any significant developments which have affected these changes?
- What percentage of those customers' business do you handle?
- How could you increase your share?

These questions help you to carry out a more detailed assessment of the needs of your largest customers. Size alone may not be sufficient grounds for concentrating customer service resources on them; there must be a positive reason for close relationships and there must be the potential within the customer's business to make the effort worth while.

Larger customers are likely to be already receiving higher levels of service to maintain or grow the business, but customer focus will require a different set of relationships and you need to be certain that you have the resources to support and develop this level of activity without putting your other major accounts at risk or upsetting the overall balance of your business.

YOUR CUSTOMERS' SUPPLY POSITION

If a customer is dependent on you for supplies that are essential to its competitive ability, that may put you in a strong position to benefit from customer focus. Use the information in your customer records and ask your salesforce to assess your supply position:

- What percentage of the product do you supply?
- How does that compare with your competitors' share?
- How important is your product to the customer's business?
- Does your product have any specific features or benefits that cannot be substituted easily?

- Is your customer's demand for the product likely to grow?
- Can you add value to the product so that the customer obtains better value for money?
- Can you introduce other customer focused services to strengthen your position?

This analysis will indicate how customer focus could benefit your business and your customer's. It will help you decide how to align your business to your customer's needs.

RESEARCHING CUSTOMER REQUIREMENTS

Supply vulnerability may not be the only consideration. Your customers may want access to your technology or your distributor network, or they may see opportunities in working together on joint projects to improve cost or performance. By researching customer requirements, you can identify other opportunities to build stronger relationships.

An industry research programme into computers in manufacturing helped to form the basis of partnership for a major computer manufacturer. The key findings of the survey were:

- Over a five-year period, the number of computer installations had risen from 40 to 70 per cent of manufacturing sites surveyed. This showed that there was still opportunity to make first-time sales by helping manufacturers to understand the need for computerisation.
- Over the same five-year period, existing users had increased their usage of computers for different applications. This indicated that a key factor in partnership would be technical support and application development to help partners make the most of their investment in computers.
- The survey highlighted the rapid growth of personal computers compared with mainframe installations. This would require a major investment in user training, therefore a partner who could offer training and implementation support would provide a major benefit.
- Computers were increasingly used for specific functions such as Computer-Aided Design and Manufacturing (CAD/CAM), so it was important that partners were able to demonstrate an understanding of manufacturing requirements.
- Integration and compatibility between different equipment sources were seen as important requirements for future purchasing decisions. Manufacturers indicated that they would either buy from a single source or buy products

that could be easily integrated. Potential partners would have to provide a broad product range or demonstrate skills in product integration.

Independent research information provides a valuable input into the development of a partnership proposal and it can also indicate the potential of different customers to provide customer focus opportunities. Independent research provides the most objective form of information to make this type of decision, but there are other ways in which you can obtain this information:

- telephone research into customer satisfaction with a recent purchase – what were the most important factors in selecting the equipment?
- telephone research into future buying requirements – what would you look for in selecting your next product?
- analysis of recent competitive purchases of products and services – what combination of support services and products is the customer buying and what does this tell you about their requirements?
- published surveys of industry buying patterns. These can provide background information to the independent commissioned research, but the quality of the information depends on the willingness of leading companies to participate.

Research into customer requirements helps to answer the question, 'would customer focus and closer working relationships help customers meet their most important requirements and, more importantly, can we meet those requirements?'

ASSESSING COMPETITIVE THREATS

Although you may recognise opportunities to grow or protect your business by building closer relationships with your customers, you may not always be in the driving seat. You may be forced into a response by competitive action but you must be sure that the actions provide you with competitive benefits as well as protection. Your market research should provide you with information on competitive activity and you can use this as a basis for analysing opportunities:

- Who are your main competitors?
- What percentage of potential partnership business do they hold?
- How long have they been dealing with the customer?
- How do your products compare with competitive offerings?
- What are your competitors' main strengths?
- Have they invested in links with customers which would make it difficult for other suppliers to make inroads?

- Have you got the skills and resources to overcome the competitive threat?
- Are any competitors making inroads into businesses where you are currently the dominant supplier?
- How do your competitors compare with the customer requirements identified in the last section?
- What are customers' attitudes towards your competitors?
- How do they compare with attitudes towards your company?

Competitive analysis helps you to identify how you can protect your most important business and, more positively, how you can strengthen your position with customers in situations where your competitors are currently holding a larger share of the business than you. To strengthen your position with a customer where competitive activity is growing, you must be certain that the investment is positive. If you build stronger links with a customer, is the customer's business growing in line with your investment? If your investment simply maintains the business at a static level, you may be missing other opportunities. If the actions you take to protect your business provide you with new opportunities, there is a strong basis for investing resources. For example, if you invest in communications or on-line ordering systems to simplify purchasing procedures and lock your customers into your business, are you likely to capture other business currently held by competitors?

Increasing the level of technical support you provide to your customers may enable you to strengthen your links with the technical department and raise your profile within the organisation. A higher technical profile could provide you with new business opportunities that were not previously available. In the same way, improvements in your own design or manufacturing processes to drive down costs or increase value for money may increase your own efficiency or provide you with the capacity to handle additional products for your customers.

UNDERSTANDING YOUR CUSTOMERS' MARKETS

As the research programme outlined earlier in the chapter showed, customers regard market understanding as an important factor in selecting suppliers. By analysing your customers' performance in the market-place, you can identify their strengths and weaknesses and put forward proposals that will enable them to improve their competitive performance. Customer information such as corporate brochures, annual reports and press information will help you to build an understanding of your customers' current achievements. You should also consider published industry surveys and research material which shows how your customers are perceived in relation to their competitors and how they meet the main requirements of their market-place.

The information will help you to build a picture of your customers' position in the market:

- What are their main markets?
- Are their markets shrinking or growing?
- What is your customers' position in the market-place?
- How has their position changed over the last five years?
- Who are your customers' main competitors?
- How are they regarded in the market-place and how has their relative position changed over the past five years?
- What are the key success factors in the market?
- What are the long-term trends in the market?
- What new technical developments will be needed to succeed in the market?
- Could innovation help your customers to succeed?
- Do your customers need to improve their quality standards or their delivery performance?
- Are your customers aiming at market leadership or an increase in share?
- Are your customers considering entry into new markets?
- Do you have skills that are relevant to the new market?

By demonstrating this understanding and showing how you can help your customers achieve their objectives, you can put forward positive proposals and build a relationship that benefits both parties.

UNDERSTANDING CUSTOMER STRATEGIES

It is equally important to understand your customers' business strategies – what is their corporate direction, how do they aim to succeed, what are their key objectives? By aligning your objectives with theirs and showing how your products or services can help them to achieve their strategic business objectives, you demonstrate that you can make an important contribution to their business. The analysis of customer strategies will help you to develop a number of scenarios for improving relationships:

- Your customers want to achieve market leadership through innovation. Your technical skills and resources can help them develop the right level of innovation without investment in their own skills.
- Your customers want to become value-for-money suppliers and succeed through competitive pricing. You can help them reduce overall costs by improving design and manufacturing costs or by handling non-core activities

cost effectively.

- Your customers want to increase their capacity so that they can compete effectively with larger competitors. You can supplement their resources by providing external skills and resources.
- Your customers want to develop a nationwide network of local branches. You can provide a basis for their network through your own local resources, cutting down on their investment and giving them a rapid start.
- Your customers want to build a strong international presence. If you have an established international network, your partners can use your local knowledge and contacts to establish their international business.
- Your customers want to rationalise their operations to concentrate on their core business. They can utilise your specialist skills to supplement their resources and allow their key staff to focus on strategic business tasks.
- Your customers want to maintain their market position by strengthening their supply position. You can provide them with a quality-assured source of supply that provides them with continuity.

This series of scenarios shows that an understanding of your customers' strategic objectives can provide you with an opportunity to build strong relationships that increase your customers' dependence on you.

ASSESSING THE VALUE OF YOUR PRODUCTS AND SERVICES

As the previous section showed, products and services that help your customers to meet their strategic business objectives can increase customer dependence. The more your customers depend on you, the stronger the relationship. These are some possible scenarios:

- You are the only supplier of a key industrial component that is vital to your customers.
- Your main competitor has gone out of business and your customer now has only a single source of supply.
- Your customer must develop new products quickly to retain and protect market share and your products are critical to their product development programme.
- Your customers have to reduce their cost base to compete effectively and your processes and services will help them to succeed.
- Your customers need to improve their levels of customer satisfaction and your products and services are vital to their success.

Identifying opportunities like this requires a detailed understanding of the customer's business and a close working relationship that allows you to focus on their problems and opportunities.

UTILISING YOUR TECHNICAL EXPERTISE

Technical strengths can be an important determining factor in building close working relationships. Access to technical expertise is one of the main reasons companies look for long-term relationships with suppliers. In assessing opportunities, you should analyse how your technical skills can help your customers. They can use your skills in a number of ways:

- to improve the performance of their own products and services by using your design and development skills. Through partnership, they may gain privileged access to your technical skills to improve their own competitive performance.
- using your technical expertise to enhance the skills of their own technical staff. By working with your technical staff, they may be able to learn new skills and techniques, and broaden their own experience so that they can make a more effective contribution to their own technical operations.
- using your technical resources to handle product development on a subcontract basis. This provides your partners with access to specialist resources or additional research and development capacity to improve the performance of their product development programmes;
- using your technical expertise to develop new products that they could not achieve themselves. This provides your customers with new technology and allows them to diversify in line with your specialist skills.
- using your skills and experience to overcome technical problems. If your customers are having recurring problems with performance and reliability, your skills can help them reduce complaints and increase customer satisfaction.
- using your design skills to improve through-life costs. By carrying out value engineering studies on your customers' products, you may be able to reduce overall costs and improve reliability by designing components that are easier to assemble and maintain.
- providing your customers with technical support and back up. If your customers have to provide their users with a technical support service, you can supplement their resources or handle the support service on their behalf.

To identify which of these technical services might be an appropriate basis for building relationships, you need to research attitudes towards your customers' products. How are they rated in industry surveys or press reviews? How do customers feel about them? Are you aware of reliability problems? How do competitors' products compare in terms of reliability and performance? Are there new industry performance standards which will be difficult to achieve without considerable technical development.

By assessing your customers' current performance and future requirements you will be able to identify areas where they might depend on your technical expertise. Your proposal can be tailored to those technical requirements.

SUMMARY

This chapter has explained how to use information on your customers to assess the potential and likely contribution of customer focus. By analysing your sales and customer information you can build a profile of your customers' business and see how customer focus could best help them. The process may be as simple as identifying your largest customers and building close working relationships to protect the business. Pressures on your customers' supply position may encourage them to pursue closer ties, while a close study of their requirements enables you to identify the key factors that determine the direction of customer focus. Published surveys and other forms of research will provide a firm basis for developing a customer focus programme. Competitive threats may make it necessary for you to strengthen customer focus, but there may be barriers if your customers' attitudes towards your competitors are more positive. By understanding your customers' strategies, their markets and their attitudes you can help to create the right environment for customer focus communications. You also need to assess your own strengths – how important are your products or your technical skills?

Self-assessment checklist

- Do you have customer information in a form that provides customer focus information?

- Do you use your salesforce to provide you with customer focus information?

- Can you identify which customers have the greatest potential?

- Are there barriers to building strong relationships with your largest customers?

- Would customer focus strengthen your position as a supplier?

- Are you in a position where your customers depend on you?

- Do you have access to industry research or other published material that will help to identify customer requirements?

- Can you carry out your own research into customer requirements?

- Do the research findings provide you with a useful basis for customer focus?

- Does competitive analysis demonstrate a need for customer focus?

- How can you use customer focus to counter the competitive threat?

- Are there any significant competitive barriers to developing close relationships?

- How well do you understand your customers' markets?

- Where can you obtain information on them?

- How would customer focus activities help your customers improve their competitive position?

- Do you have information on your customers' strategies?

- How well do your customers' strategies fit with your own business plans?

- Would closer relationships help your customers to achieve their objectives more easily?

- How important are your products to your customers?

- Can you use your supply position to build strong relationships?

- How important are your technical skills to your customers?

- Would close working relationships enable your customers to make better use of your technical skills?

- Would your services enable your customers to improve their own technical performance?

5

FOCUSING STAFF ON YOUR CUSTOMERS

How can role reversal help your staff focus on customer service? If audits and internal research reveal low levels of awareness of customer needs, you have to raise awareness and make sure that staff respond to that understanding. The problem is compounded when a manufacturer is dealing at arms length with customers through a distributor or retail outlet. The manufacturer has no direct control over retail staff and poor performance at retail level can damage customer relations.

As part of their overall customer care strategy, Ford developed a range of customer focus actions that included a programme called 'Put Yourself in Their Shoes'. This programme used reports from customer surveys that described common problems with service from the local dealership. The report was described in full and the member of staff was given guidelines on improving performance. The programme was wide ranging and involved all levels of staff within dealership, including:

- service technicians
- service receptionists
- parts managers
- parts counter staff
- dealer principal.

The programme was the forerunner of the Customer Satisfaction Performance Programme which measured the performance of individual dealerships and departments in those areas which had been identified as crucial to customer satisfaction. Customer satisfaction programmes are described in more detail later in the book, but a programme like 'Put yourself in their shoes' can prove to be a valuable forerunner to a full customer satisfaction programme.

WHERE CUSTOMER FOCUS IS IMPORTANT

'Put Yourself in Their Shoes' is applicable to any business where staff actions impact on customer service. It is particularly appropriate for staff who are not directly in touch with customers and who may be overlooked in a customer care training programme. In a manufacturing company this might include accounts clerks who produce inaccurate invoices, warehouse staff who pick the wrong parts, or departmental managers who refuse to co-operate in allocating resources to customer-facing activities.

In a service business, it is the people who deliver the service – the technicians and engineers – who are crucial. In some service businesses, they are dealing directly with customers – engineers on site – but in the car business, for example, they are 'hidden away', never exposed to a customer. Any customer complaints are filtered through a series of receptionists and supervisors, and the customer never gets an opportunity to talk directly with the service technician. Enlightened dealers who recognise the problem have brought service technicians 'out to the front' to talk to customers or have provided customers with viewing areas where they can watch their cars being serviced. Dealers who expose their service staff in this way and made them accountable report that the exercise has a high motivational benefit.

The same process can be applied to professional services where there is a traditional layer of account management between the customer and the service provider. In advertising, for example, the account director, followed by the account manager and an account executive, with perhaps a client services director as well, stand between the customer and the creative team who develop the advertisements. The creative process also filters down through a creative group head to a creative director to a writer and art director, so the opportunities for low customer awareness are high.

WHEN THE PROGRAMME IS VALUABLE

It is the barriers between the customer and the people who provide the service that make programmes like 'Put yourself in their shoes' so important. These are the business scenarios that indicate when a programme is necessary:

● There are high levels of customer complaint with standards of service.
● The complaints can be attributed to poor performance by staff who are not in direct contact with customers, although some of them may be.
● The problems cannot be overcome by quality actions or by change to the physical processes.

- The problems are rooted in poor customer attitudes or a lack of understanding of customer needs.
- There is no mechanism for the key staff to learn about customer needs; the staff are trained in technical skills, but they have no experience of customer care.
- Customer concerns can be identified through surveys and questionnaires, and it is possible to get specific comments from customers.
- Training and other customer actions can be used to improve performance and raise levels of customer satisfaction.
- The market is competitive and the product or service delivery can easily be imitated by competitors; the only differentiating factor is the quality service and customer care.
- Customer care can be easily communicated to customers and will help to develop the service to a higher standard.

These business scenarios can be applied to a wide range of businesses and help to identify where the customer focus should be placed.

AIMS OF THE PROGRAMME

Ford's overall aim was to improve the quality of service available through dealerships as a means of building long-term customer satisfaction. The objectives of an initiative such as 'Put yourself in their shoes' include:

- to raise overall levels of customer satisfaction
- to ensure that individual outlets are able to deliver a consistent standard of service
- to raise awareness of the importance of customer care among staff at all levels
- to make staff aware of customer needs
- to ensure that customer focus is built into all training activities and business processes
- to ensure that customer care activities can be measured.

PROGRAMME OPERATION

'Put yourself in their shoes' was a wide-ranging programme that covered all aspects of Ford dealer operations. The programme began with a process of research using customer complaints and customer feedback as a means of identifying the main causes of concern. The complaints were addressed to individual dealers and communicated to Ford. The complaints were analysed by Ford and formed patterns so that the company could identify where the main problems were originating. The problems were segmented into the following areas:

- parts department
- service department
- bodyshop
- pre-delivery inspection department.

The programme also identified that the following people would be involved in the process:

- parts manager
- parts supervisor
- parts counter staff
- service manager
- service receptionist
- service supervisor
- service technician.

It was important that senior management in the dealerships were aware of the process of customer focus and were committed to its success because they would have to allocate time and resources to implement the improvement programme. The medium for getting the information to target staff was brochures and videos with training guides to support the material.

The programme was initially launched to the dealer body through a series of regional business meetings followed by sales visits to individual dealerships. At the regional business meetings, dealer principals – the senior management team – were given a background briefing on the importance of the programme and given individual launch packs that explained how the programmes were to be operated.

The company also introduced a series of complementary initiatives to add a competitive element to the programme. Dealership staff who reached the required standard in their own activities were invited to join specialist staff guilds and compete against each other to be 'Service Receptionist of the Year' or 'Technician of the Year'. This inter-dealer rivalry was important to the long-term success of the programme because it paved the way for the introduction of nationwide customer focus standards in the future. The regional business meetings helped to build commitment to the programme at senior level and paved the way for the individual dealer launch.

The programme was too important just to send a brochure and video to dealers and let them get on with it. Sales staff who were responsible for dealer liaison and development visited each dealer to hold an introductory session and to discuss an implementation plan with each dealership. The programme was introduced to key members of staff who had been identified earlier in the programme.

A video which explained the overall aims of the programme was used to introduce the sessions and the Ford representative then worked with individual groups to help them identify ways in which they could improve their performance. The basis of the improvement programmes was a selection of customer comments which cover common faults with the product or the service, 'the ashtray was full and I'm a non-smoker', 'they left grease all over the steering wheel', 'I found the same fault even though I had described it in detail to the service receptionist'.

BENEFITS OF THE PROGRAMME

The programme enabled Ford to build a commitment to customer care among staff who felt that they had little to do with customers and laid the groundwork for future customer care programmes that were targeted at different groups of staff. By using customer comments directly, they helped staff to look at their work from the customer's point of view and to treat each customer as an individual. The programme also encouraged an attitude of competition between different groups of staff and this allowed progress to be measured. Comparing the customer care rating of different departments or different dealerships allows Ford to take action to improve under-performing dealerships and to reward achievement.

Customers benefit because they receive higher standards of service and they can be confident that their concerns will be recognised. By telling the company about their problems, they are encouraging and receiving a positive response. They can expect that their cars will be taken care of and returned in the best possible condition.

PUTTING THE PROGRAMME INTO OPERATION

These are the key stages in putting a programme like this into operation:

- Identify the people who are the target for the programme.
- Use customer research to assess the planned outcome of the programme.
- Develop a training programme that will improve staff performance.
- Encourage staff to develop their own action programmes.
- Measure and reward improvements in performance.
- Provide a basis for comparison between different groups of staff.
- Get the commitment of managers to support the programme by demonstrating business benefits.

- Provide support and resources to implement the programme at local level.
- Ensure that customer queries and concerns receive a positive response.
- Involve customers in the process of improving standards and keep them informed of progress.

SUMMARY

'Put yourself in their shoes' is a programme that helps staff understand customers by directly relaying customer comments to 'back-room staff'. The customer comments represent common problems in customer relations and encourage the staff to recognise their customers' concerns and take action. Action programmes should be put into place to improve performance and there should be a basis for measuring progress and comparative performance. The programme enables customer focus to be introduced throughout an organisation and helps to raise standards of customer service.

Self-assessment checklist

- Can you identify opportunities to raise customer awareness among all levels of staff?
- Is lack of customer awareness pulling down customer standards?
- What are the critical activities that impact on customer satisfaction?
- Can you encourage your customers to put their concerns in writing, and can you promise them a positive response?
- What other mechanisms can you use to obtain customer feedback?
- Can you utilise existing training programmes to improve performance?
- How can you measure and compare performance between different groups?

6

SETTING CUSTOMER FOCUS STANDARDS

**Customer care has become one of the most important issues facing business-
es in every market. Customer care programmes come under a number of
different titles – customer service, customer satisfaction, customer focus,
customer-oriented. Their common theme is meeting the customers' requirements and ensuring that all aspects of the business contribute to customer
satisfaction. The intention is to build repeat business. If customers are
satisfied with the product and the standards of service they receive, they will
return to the same outlet again and again – for major or minor purchases.**

WHEN CUSTOMER FOCUS STANDARDS ARE IMPORTANT

Most companies are now operating a customer care programme of some descrip-
tion, but the problems of running a successful programme are multiplied when
the same programme is operated through a number of different outlets. Inconsistent customer care performance can have a negative effect on customer perceptions. Petrol companies, for example, know that every time a customer walks into
one of their outlets, wherever they are in the country, they should expect to
receive the same standards of service. Nationwide consistency is essential when
customers are likely to visit multiple outlets – one poor performance can threaten
the customer's perception of the entire operation. However, the same principle
can be applied to multi-site opportunities even when customers are likely to use
only one site.

These are some of the scenarios where customer focus standards would be
important:

- Customer needs can be defined.
- Consistent standards need to be applied throughout an organisation.
- Customer needs can be converted to a customer standard.

- Customer standards can be measured.
- The company wants to demonstrate commitment to customer care.

APPROACHES TO CUSTOMER FOCUS

Customer care has two aspects:

- the physical means of delivering customer service
- the attitude of staff.

A company wishing to improve its standards of customer care could set up a customer care hotline to handle queries or complaints – that would be the physical part of the equation; but if the staff who manned the hotline were unsympathetic, the customer care benefit could be lost. Anyone who wishes to implement an effective customer care strategy should look for a balance between the two. It is also important to recognise that management and staff at every level affect customer care and loyalty. Programmes that build a customer care attitude must operate at every level. Customer care can operate in a variety of ways:

- offering customers the products and services that reflect their real needs
- offering greater levels of convenience which make it easier for customers to buy from your outlets
- providing a customer service centre where customers can make enquiries or complain
- improving the overall quality of service so that customers recognise a change in performance.

The most important aspect of any programme is to focus people on customer care and this can be achieved in a number of ways:

- running customer focus panels to identify customer needs and discuss their views on the quality of service
- issuing customer focus standards to ensure consistent standards
- introducing customer care programmes which give a high profile to the whole process of customer care
- running customer care programmes to ensure that all staff understand the importance of customer care
- introducing customer satisfaction ratings to measure how well outlets are performing
- operating customer satisfaction incentive schemes to reward outlets who have achieved the highest levels of customer satisfaction

- integrating customer care activities into business and marketing programmes to ensure that the whole business is driven by customer needs
- using customer care to build customer loyalty.

RESEARCHING CUSTOMER FOCUS STANDARDS

It would be very easy to introduce customer care slogans and encourage staff to demonstrate customer care, but the actions would be wasted without an understanding of what customers actually needed. As so many observers have pointed out, 'customer care is more than wearing a smile and saying have a nice day'. Customer care is meeting customers' real needs and the hardest part is to identify those needs.

One way is to use a technique known as focus panels where customers and an interviewer meet to discuss their requirements and attitudes to the service that is offered. Eaton House Consultants run a number of customer focus panels for major petrol retailers. The customers in this case are motorists and they include a cross-section of a petrol station's customer base:

- business travellers
- delivery drivers
- long-distance lorry drivers
- domestic drivers
- elderly drivers
- handicapped drivers.

The aim was to find out what each of these motorists wanted from a petrol service station. The key issues were convenience of opening hours, ease of access, number of pumps, location, payment facilities, customer facilities such as toilets and drinks, and the availability of other products such as snacks, motoring products and, increasingly, the range of other products available on the forecourt. The information provided by the motorists' panel showed the retailer the direction in which he could expand his business and provided a valuable indication of the areas which needed improvement.

The second stage of the focus panel was to review the findings of the panel with the management team and to develop an action plan to make any improvements which had been identified. The information was also used as a basis for national planning. By putting together the information from panels around the country, the head office team were able to identify regional and national patterns in consumer requirements. This provided a valuable basis for planning national forecourt development programmes and providing the right level of regional and local support. The focus panels were held on a regional basis and this proved a valuable method of monitoring customers' response to the improvements that had been made at the suggestion of earlier focus panels. By showing that they were prepared to respond to motorists' concerns, the retailer was able to demonstrate high levels of customer care.

This particular programme enabled detailed customer focus programmes to be developed at local level and integrated with national customer focus programmes. The research programme carried out by Glen Carter Associates for a European automotive components manufacturer shows how the same principles can be applied at a pan-European level. Comments from customers given in a separate survey showed that they were having difficulty in obtaining information from dealers on the company's range of accessories. When they were able to obtain copies of the accessories catalogue, customers found them difficult to use and, as a result, their overall levels of satisfaction were reduced. The research also indicated that the response to the accessories catalogue varied by location.

As the accessories programme was an important factor in maintaining contact between vehicle sales, the company decided to commission more detailed research into the customers' requirements for an accessories catalogue. The researchers decided to concentrate on two main questions:

- How easy did customers find it to get information on accessories?
- What sort of information did they need?

On the question of getting information, customers commented that they had to ask for catalogues and, where they were on display, they were uncertain whether they had to pay for them. Commenting on the contents of the catalogue, customers were divided over the question of whether accessories should be shown by model; many felt that prices should be shown and most were confused about the process of ordering accessories. Customers were also shown competitive accessories literature and asked for their response to content and quality. The research programme was carried out across seven European countries and the results, unsurprisingly, revealed significant differences between markets.

The company's response was to develop a series of accessories brochures incorporating local variations. The brochures were initially produced by model range with a simple ordering system based on product numbers. Each of the 17 language variations contained model information that was specific to that territory. Prices were included or omitted depending on the response of the local market and the views of dealers in that territory. The content of the brochure was now tailored more closely to the needs of customers in each market.

To ensure that customers were able to obtain the information easily within dealerships, the company developed a merchandising and incentive programme which included prominent displays for the customer, direct mail aimed at local customers and a structured incentive programme based on sales of accessories. As a result of this customer research, the company was able to introduce an accessories programme which reflected customer needs as well as the specific needs of local markets.

SETTING CUSTOMER FOCUS STANDARDS

Using focus panels is a good way to build an understanding of customer needs. If that understanding can be built into customer focus standards which determine how the business is run at local level, it will help to improve the consistency of performance and demonstrate to customers that the company is responding to their requirements. Many franchised and independent distributors have to conform to operating requirements as part of their distributor agreement. Typically, these would cover the size of the premises, facilities, stock levels, head count, capital funding, management skills and training requirements to ensure that the branch was able to provide the level of service covered by their agreement.

An increasing number of companies are introducing customer focus standards as part of their agreement to improve levels of customer satisfaction. The Post Office, for example, is moving many of its main Post Offices from central high street positions to new locations within large retail outlets or to out-of-town shopping centres. Part of the reason for the change is to reduce the cost of maintaining an expensive town centre position, but they are also taking the opportunity to move to premises that are more convenient for their customers and to improve the quality of service.

Many were relocated within retail outlets and were able to offer longer opening hours, plus the convenience of offering their customers the chance to do other shopping at the same time. The out of town locations offered even greater convenience with adequate parking, wheelchair access, spacious premises and the same opportunities for longer opening hours and one-stop shopping. These retailing developments, together with future developments in counter automation, training and an increasing range of products and services were at the heart of the Post Office's drive to become a more customer focused organisation serving the needs of the local market.

A number of American-style pizza home delivery services are run as franchise operations and they aim to improve the quality and consistency of their service by introducing customer focus standards. They realise that, in a fiercely competitive market, they have to establish a strong brand identity and that identity is based not just on the quality of the pizza but on the quality of service. Many of the operators offer a guaranteed home delivery time backed by a full refund if they fail to meet the time. They want to attract customers by offering the convenience of home delivery, but they have suffered in the past from inconsistent delivery performance with the pizzas arriving unacceptably late or arriving cold. The promise to deliver on time or provide a refund is a powerful motivator for the local staff since failure hits directly at their profit levels.

Direct Line Insurance has introduced high levels of convenience and rapid response into the car insurance market and shows that a successful and profitable business can be built on customer focus standards. The company accepts enquiries through a well-trained customer reception centre. The customers are guided through a series of simple questions and the respondent then provides an immediate quotation. If the customer wishes to proceed, the respondent issues immediate cover without any further administration or form filling. Claims are handled in a similar way. The result for the customer is a service that is simple, responsive, convenient and good value for money. Direct Line have the advantage that they handle incoming enquiries centrally, but other organisations can use the same principles to establish a customer focused service.

BENEFITS

Customer focus standards help to implement consistent standards of customer service and care throughout an organisation. By isolating the elements that customers feel are most important, a company can concentrate its resources on meeting those requirements. Customer focus standards provide a visible commitment to customers that their needs are important. To customers, the standards provide an assurance of quality which means that they can expect the highest levels of service whenever they deal with the company.

KEY MANAGEMENT ACTIONS

- Commit adequate resources to the programme.
- Identify key customer concerns through research.
- Establish standards for each of the areas identified by research.
- Provide support for action programmes to improve performance.
- Develop techniques for measuring performance against standards.
- Use the standards as a means of controlling the performance of different outlets.

SUMMARY

This chapter has shown how high standards of customer care are essential to building customer satisfaction and loyalty at local level and looked at the different ways in which customer care can be delivered. Customer focus panels, for example, help suppliers identify their customers expectations and the chapter shows how these expectations can be used to develop customer focus standards which can contribute to consistent standards of customer care.

Self-assessment checklist

- Does your company have a clearly-defined customer care policy?

- How do your customers rate your customer care performance?

- Do you have a clear process for dealing with complaints or queries?

- Could you utilise customer focus panels to raise awareness of customer expectations within your organisation?

- What are the important factors you would seek customers' views on?

- Do you have a set of defined customer focus standards?

- What impact would customer focus standards have on your business?

7

IMPROVING CONVENIENCE FOR CUSTOMERS

When the Post Office relocated some of its main branches away from traditional town centre sites to out-of-town retail developments or into other central retail sites, it was criticised for changing a long-standing service, but it was able to counter that criticism by pointing out that it had improved convenience for a wide range of domestic and business users as well as taking the opportunity to benefit from the introduction of new services and new technology.

This chapter looks at ways of improving convenience for the customer and uses examples mainly from the retail sector. Longer opening hours, more convenient locations, better parking or public transport links and integration of leisure and shopping activities have helped to make shopping a more convenient experience.

However, the same principles can be applied to business and service industries. Components manufacturers, for example, who locate their factories in close proximity to key customers so that both can enjoy the benefits of closer working relationships, or the example of Eastern Electricity who make their customer help centre available 24 hours a day for any type of enquiry. The intention in all cases is to make it as easy as possible for customers to use the service. Automatic Teller Machines make banking and building society services available 24 hours a day while 'open all hours' corner shops enjoy a powerful neighbourhood competitive advantage over traditional shops.

WHEN IS THE PROGRAMME SUITABLE?

The convenience approach can be valuable in a number of business scenarios:

- The company is losing business to competitors who offer more convenient forms of service, longer opening hours or a more convenient location.

- The company wishes to attract a broader audience who are not able to use the service in its current form – car service customers, for example, who use their cars throughout the week are offered Saturday service or overnight service, or service at the local rail station car park.
- The company wants to make convenience a major selling platform – for example offering customers a no-appointment necessary service or 24-hour opening so that customers can use the service whenever they need to.
- Customers are demanding better standards of service and their needs can be used to develop and operate customer focus standards.
- The opportunity exists to introduce higher standards of customer service by taking advantage of new technology or new facilities – for example by relocating a factory to take advantage of Just-in-Time techniques.
- Technology allows the service to be extended or relocated to improve convenience – the introduction of home shopping services or the location of cash dispensers at airports, motorway service areas and retail centres.
- Convenience is identified as the most important factor in customer research.

SETTING PROGRAMME OBJECTIVES

In introducing a convenience programme, companies should set the following objectives:

- to offer customers the highest standards of convenience
- to develop a competitive advantage through a focus on convenience
- to meet standards of convenience that reflect customer needs
- to achieve best practice in the convenience that is offered
- to strengthen customer relationships through the introduction of convenience services.

THE PROGRAMME

When the Post Office was carrying out a review of its strategy for main branch location, it carried out research into customer needs and changing retail patterns. Many of the main post offices were located in central high street areas with sub-post offices located in neighbourhoods to provide a local service. The main post offices provided a wider range of services and were key to the Post Office's future development. Sub-post offices provided essential Royal Mail, payment and savings facilities but did not offer the broader range of services.

Future developments would require a greater use of technology and would put a different emphasis on space utilisation with the development of post shops and other special retailing activities within the Post Office. In many cases, the traditional sites did not have the potential for conversion or expansion and this would limit future change and growth. The opportunity to rebuild or relocate in traditional town centre areas was also difficult because of the property costs.

More important, consumer habits were changing. Traffic congestion, parking restrictions and a reduction in public transport made it more difficult for customers to make a quick visit to the Post Office – the visit would have to be part of a wider shopping trip. Customers were also making extensive use of out-of-town shopping centres where all the important food and retail outlets were to be found with easy access by car and public transport. Although the Post Office recognised the potential consumer benefits of relocation in terms of improving customer service and convenience, it was also aware of its responsibilities to specific groups within the community, particularly the elderly or people who would not be able to get to the new locations easily by private or public transport.

The Post Office was seen as abandoning its traditional role and there was a concern among local opinion formers that this was a change in direction. As part of the development programme, the Post Office undertook a process of local consultation and information to ensure that their proposals were fully acceptable. A briefing pack for local opinion formers, aimed at politicians, local councillors, trade associations and consumer groups explained the overall benefits:

- The new branches would have better parking facilities and would be located close to public transport.
- Opening hours would be longer and the branches would provide a wider range of services.
- The new offices would offer other convenience facilities, including larger counter areas, a more open aspect, disabled access and facilities such as telephones and photobooths.
- In many cases the post offices were located within a store and operated as a franchise. The store owner would provide the facilities and the staff who would be trained in Post Office procedures and wear Post Office uniforms. The Post Office within a store was seen as an important customer benefit, cutting down the number of separate shopping visits a customer had to make and offering the advantages of one-stop shopping.
- Many of the new post offices would incorporate new technology which would allow the Post Office to deliver higher standards of service and deliver a wider range of services.

The same process of convenience can be applied to the retail sector. A regional shopping centre such as Lakeside in Essex reflects all the aspects of convenience.

The centre is located close to the M25 motorway network and the Dartford crossing, making access easy from London and the Home Counties. Local customers have fast access routes through dual carriageways, special access roads and effective public transport.

The centre is built on a large site with adequate free parking and contains all the most popular retail outlets under one roof with covered access to all large and small stores.

Refreshments are available throughout the centre and entertainments, in the form of cinemas and other leisure activities are an integral part of the centre so that groups or families can use the centre for different purposes. Larger specialist superstores for electrical goods, carpets, computers, toys and other consumer durables are located on an adjacent retail centre, extending the concept of one-stop shopping. The stores feature longer opening hours and many make use of the latest electronic point of sale facilities to ensure that shopping is convenient and easy.

BENEFITS OF THE PROGRAMME

The benefits to the organisation introducing the convenience programmes include the ability to:

- compete with organisations offering more convenient forms of service
- attract a broader audience who are not able to use the service in its current form
- meet customer demands for better standards of service
- introduce higher standards of customer service by taking advantage of new technology or new facilities
- allow the service to be extended or relocated to improve convenience
- build higher levels of satisfaction and strengthen customer relationships.

Customers obtain a better standard of service and the service is focused on their needs. They can use the service at a time that is convenient to them and they have greater choice.

KEY MANAGEMENT ACTIONS

- Research and identify the convenience factors customers feel are most important.
- Audit your current levels of convenience and compare them with customer needs and competitive offerings.
- Establish a set of customer focus standards for the new service.

- Consult customers and other influencers if significant change is involved.
- Assess the potential of new technology to improve convenience further.
- Identify the staff training requirements to ensure that customers receive the highest standards of service.
- Introduce measures to monitor performance against the new standards.
- Look for opportunities to introduce new services or products that take advantage of the new facilities.

SUMMARY

This chapter has looked at ways of improving convenience for the customer and shown how companies in the retail sector have used factors such as longer opening hours, more convenient locations, better parking or public transport links and integration of leisure and shopping activities to make shopping a more convenient experience. The same principles can be applied to business and service industries by building closer working relationships and making it easier for customers to do business. In many cases, new technology can be used to improve aspects of convenience or to launch new services that help attract a different audience.

Self-assessment checklist

- How important is customer convenience to your business?
- How do you compare with your competitors?
- What are the key convenience factors?
- What level of change will be required to improve convenience?
- Can convenience be improved by training or will it require physical changes to the way you deliver service?
- Can technology help to improve convenience?
- Would convenience factors build closer working relationships with customers?
- Would the changes in service allow you to move into new market sectors?
- Can the convenience factors be measured and used to control your operations?

- Are you able to maintain consistent standards of convenience throughout your business or will there be variables?

- Are your customers aware of the changes in your service?

8

TALKING DIRECT TO CUSTOMERS

The essence of an effective customer focus programme is that companies understand their customers' needs and provide a level of service that is tailored directly to them. To communicate that precise message effectively, the most powerful medium available to companies is direct marketing.

DIRECT MARKETING

Targeting individual customers

Direct marketing is a form of communication in which individual messages are sent to individual customers – direct mail letters are the best known form of direct marketing and a simple example illustrates the difference between advertising, which aims to reach the widest possible audience at the lowest cost per contact, and direct mail which aims at one-to-one contact.

A lawnmower manufacturer runs a national advertising campaign to attract professional users.

> The Greengrow Mower is the mower for the professional user; it produces a superb finish quickly and easily, and is guaranteed for long reliable operation.

This advertisement communicates the key benefits to the professional groundsman, but the direct mail letter is targeted precisely at an individual user and it makes a very specific offer. It shows that the company understands individual needs and is completely focused.

> As the head groundsman of County Park, you will be aware of the pressure that Any Town Corporation is putting on all departments to reduce their operating costs. The new Greengrow Mower has been proved in tests to cut a cricket pitch 15 per cent faster than any competitive mower and still produce a superb finish. You not only reduce your labour costs, we have also increased the service interval so that your maintenance costs are lower. We are willing to offer you a five per cent discount on the purchase price because you are a loyal customer and we will offer you a guaranteed part

exchange price for your old models. Bob Smith, your local distributor, will be contacting you next week to discuss terms, but if you would like a demonstration in the meantime, please contact our national enquiry centre and they will arrange for a visit within 48 hours.

The key to the success of that programme is an understanding of the customer and the right level of information on that customer's needs. The database management needed to achieve that kind of targeting is described in more detail later in this chapter. Direct marketing can be a powerful weapon because it enables companies to talk to their customers on their own terms.

Customising communications

When ICL introduced the Customer Reception Centre, a single point of contact for customers throughout the country, they realised that branches would be reluctant to lose day-to-day contact with their local customers, so they balanced this with a programme of regular customer care visits which enabled the branch to take a proactive role in communications with customers. The first stage in the process was a direct mail shot which included a brochure on the benefits of the new central Customer Reception Centre, together with a personalised letter from the local branch manager explaining the changing and more positive role of the branch. The brochure itself was customised with a map showing the location of the branch, and the letter was addressed to customers individually. A mailing like this had the benefit of centralised design and production to ensure quality and consistency, but it bore the name of the local outlet to ensure the right level of contact.

A more conventional use of direct marketing is the specific offer to customers of a local outlet. The Spring Motoring Check is one of a range of seasonal offers made by car dealers to build local service business. Customers are offered a free safety check, plus a report on any service or maintenance needed, together with an estimate. Each dealership nominates its own prices or offers within overall guidelines and is able to make a special seasonal gift offer as an added incentive. The mail shots are produced centrally and overprinted with the detailed local information before central distribution to produce a tailored local offer.

The British Airways Speedwing Training programme, which is described in the next chapter, relies on carefully targeted direct mail to provide each of the local travel agents in the network with a customised training programme. The training agency develops a database with all the information on local skills and business requirements, and then mails details of individual training programmes to each travel agent. The travel agent only receives relevant information and does not have to sift through unwanted information.

Supporting sector marketing

Although the British Airways programme is designed to improve relationships between a company and its agents, the same technique can be used to support travel agents marketing to their customers. Galileo, a company owned by a group of international airlines, provides computerised information and reservation systems to travel agents. Using the Galileo system, a travel agent can offer customers a fast efficient service that is vital to winning and retaining business. To help travel agents communicate the benefits to their customers, Galileo developed a series of direct mail programmes aimed at different sectors of the market such as business travellers, package holiday customers and special interest holidays. A series of letters and offers is available to the travel agents for customisation on their own personal computer systems and the letters have identified variables for modification by the travel agent.

The programme can be easily modified to suit the individual travel agent's own customer profile. If, for example, the agent handles a high level of business travel and the agent has information on the travelling patterns of its customers, it could offer special deals on car hire, hotels and entertainment for the travellers' regular destinations. It could also ensure that individual business travellers took full advantage of the 'frequent flyer' offers made by many of their major airlines.

Air UK, an independent airline based at Stansted, provided their travel agents with a customised mailing service based on knowledge of business travel destinations. They had identified, through analysis of customer patterns, that a high level of business was coming from companies in financial engineering and the oil business using regional airports to fly staff to and from London via Stansted. The company ran a series of advertisements in local newspapers within the catchment areas of the regional airports to build the perception of Air UK and Stansted as the most efficient way to meet domestic and regional travel and then worked in conjunction with local travel agents to develop a direct marketing programme aimed at the most important market sectors.

The travel agents identified the companies within their regions who fitted the travelling profile – head office or branch in the region and other branches or head office in London or one of the regional airports. They mailed these companies introductory information on the Air UK service and offered to carry out an analysis of their UK travel requirements. The agent then operated a regular mailing programme which included special offers for regular travellers, together with personalised gifts. This direct marketing was integrated with the national and regional advertising campaign and demonstrates the value of co-operation between an operator and agents.

DATABASE MANAGEMENT

The key to the success of all these programmes is detailed knowledge of the customer base so that the offers and information can be tailored to individual marketing programmes. The most efficient way to handle this is to maintain a central database of all customers and use database management techniques to manage the mailing list.

Contents of the database

The database would contain the names and addresses of customers, together with variable information such as:

- purchasing patterns
- size of expenditure
- type of purchase
- number of employees
- other variations depending on the type of business.

Some examples illustrate how the database can be utilised to produce targeted mailing lists. The title describes the product and the list represents different members of the target audience:

Travel agency training services

- all travel agencies
- agencies belonging to a multiple group
- independent agencies
- agencies with a turnover in excess of . . .
- agencies with less than . . . staff
- sales staff responsible for business travel
- sales staff responsible for holiday travel
- middle managers with budget responsibility for training
- staff with less than one year's travel agency experience
- staff with specific qualifications.

Travel agency customers

- business travellers
- leisure travellers

- special interest leisure travellers
- long-haul travellers
- domestic/European business travellers
- frequent flyers who cover more than . . . miles per year
- first class leisure travellers.

Car dealership

- private owners
- business users
- fleet operators
- fleet operators with more than . . . vehicles
- new car buyers in their third year of ownership
- used car buyers
- older drivers
- service customers
- bodyshop customers.

The database can be broken down into categories which correspond to market sectors and the categories can become increasingly specific.

Building the database

Information for the database can be gathered from a number of sources, including:

- customer sales records
- replies to advertisements
- responses to special offers or invitations
- applications for membership
- market research.

The initial database is unlikely to be complete and provide information in the most suitable format, so companies who wish to benefit from direct marketing run special campaigns to gather appropriate information. For example, an invitation to an open evening or a prize draw would require customers to provide information that is essential for the database.

SUMMARY

The ability to communicate with customers on an individual basis is important to a customer focused company. Tailored communications enable a company to address individual customer concerns and make offers to match their precise needs. Direct marketing is the main communications technique; customer information is held on a database and enhanced to provide a detailed picture of individual purchasing patterns. Groups of customers with similar purchasing potential can be selected for individual communications that are more effective than broadcast advertising.

Self-assessment checklist

- How do you currently communicate with customers?
- Are you able to address their individual needs and interests?
- Do you have sufficient information on their purchasing patterns to build a customer database?
- Could you use database information to improve the performance of your marketing communications programmes?

9

ALIGNING SERVICES TO CUSTOMER NEEDS

In the business-to-business sector, the way a company delivers support material can help to improve relationships with customers and distributors. This chapter describes how Speedwing Training, part of British Airways, developed a customised training support programme that was tailored to the individual needs of local travel agents. The travel agents were able to use the customised training programmes to meet their own business objectives and therefore the programmes were much more valuable.

THE IMPORTANCE OF CUSTOMISED SUPPORT SERVICES

Local training support is an integral part of retail development, but its importance is often overlooked. Companies assume that it is sufficient to apply a single national training support policy to every outlet in a network and leave the outlet to make the best of this. The assumption is that the outlets are simply smaller versions of head office and operate in exactly the same way. This denies the real benefit of using local outlets because the local outlet is the supplier's 'personal presence' in the local market and should be encouraged to develop their individual skills.

There are a number of important benefits in this approach:

- Local outlets understand their local market and can identify changing requirements quickly.
- They are aware of local competitors and can take individual actions to deal with competitive threats.
- They can build close and personal working relationships with individual customers, essential in building and retaining long-term business.
- They can use local knowledge to tailor products or services to the local market.
- They can build small effective teams to operate flexibly in the changing conditions of the local market.

This has implications for the development and marketing of local training programmes. Training must take account of these local variations and should be tailored to the needs of individual branches. This chapter explains how Speedwing Training used an extensive customer research programme as the basis for customising its own local training programmes.

WHEN CUSTOMISED SUPPORT IS IMPORTANT

There are a number of scenarios when this customised support would be appropriate:

- Support is an integral part of the business relationship.
- Individual customers or branches have different business profiles and a single, uniform support policy would not be appropriate.
- Customised support would help to strengthen business relationships.
- Customised support would help the customer or distributor improve standards of service to consumers.

PROGRAMME OBJECTIVES

- Provide the right level of support to local travel agents to help them develop their local business.
- Build stronger relationships with travel agents to secure their loyalty.
- Ensure that local outlets enjoy the highest levels of training support.
- Develop a training service that is focused on individual customer needs.

BACKGROUND

To help you understand the importance of local training, this section looks at the changing role of local branches; they must now operate in the same way as independent retail outlets, utilising the full range of retailing techniques.

Many of the significant changes in this area can be found in the travel sector. Local branch performance is important to two parties – the travel companies who market their products through travel agencies and the organisation which owns the network of agencies. Although the aim of both parties is to improve turnover and profit through each branch, their priorities are different:

- The travel companies want to ensure that branches understand their products and their markets, actively sell their products, offer their products rather than those of competitors and administer the transactions with customers efficiently. If they succeed in getting that level of response from each branch, they will have an efficient local marketing operation for their products, supplementing their own direct sales efforts.

- The owners of the network want to ensure that they can offer their customers the widest range of products and the highest standards of service. They must win distribution rights from travel companies to build up their own product portfolio and they must ensure that individual portfolios do not create an imbalance in their overall service. In order to expand, the owners must take on a broader portfolio of services and they must provide an efficient positive service on each one.

THE NEED TO DEVELOP BRANCH SKILLS

The key change in performance comes from recognising that each branch is a retail outlet, not an administrative office. It is no longer sufficient to open the doors and wait for customers to come in. A travel agency, a bank or a building society, or any 'branch office' has the potential to be a sales outlet.

The biggest change over the last five or six years has been the physical layout and appearance of the branch office. The traditional counter service, which was the only 'front' to the business, has been replaced by open-plan sales and reception areas which put the customer first. In the travel agency, the emphasis is on merchandising, good display of the products available and skilled staff who are able to advise and sell to customers as well as taking their orders. That means the managers and the staff within the travel agency must understand the importance of good display and effective customer reception.

Any organisation that wants to realise the marketing potential of its branch network must first change the culture of the network before providing support services. These physical and cultural changes in the local branch have been accompanied by a change in the responsibilities of staff from administration to sales. Technology has speeded up many of the routine administrative procedures and freed staff for customer-facing duties.

In the travel agency, for example, computerised travel information and reservation systems mean that the time-consuming tasks of locating flights, checking availability, calculating discounts, ordering tickets, and making reservations can all be handled on screen in a very short period of time. The accounting and administration that supports these operations – issuing tickets, billing customers, charging the travel and putting the transaction on to the accounting systems – had also been handled manually, but can now be handled on the same computer.

The computer not only cuts down the back-office duties, it also provides sales information that can be used to identify national opportunities. For example, customer information is readily available through the computer so that staff can provide an informed response to travel requests and can also identify previous buying patterns so that they can sell additional products and services such as car hire, hotels and onward travel when a customer orders a ticket. The emphasis is changing from merely handling requests efficiently to delivering additional levels of customer satisfaction.

AN OPPORTUNITY TO IMPROVE CUSTOMER SERVICE

This change in methods of service and the increase in customer contact gives branch offices the opportunity to sell a greater range of products and services to their customers. By gaining a better understanding of customer needs, staff can offer them a tailored package. For example, the regular business traveller can be offered the extra services described in the previous section and can also be kept up to date with new offers and services as they become available. A good sales representative keeps customers informed about faster journeys, better facilities with different airlines or travel operators, better deals on car hire or hotels, or bonuses for frequent travel, and wins business through that. Compare the business opportunities that this presents with a situation where the branch office simply processes the customer's order.

RESEARCHING LOCAL TRAINING REQUIREMENTS

When Speedwing Training was developing its customer service training package for travel agencies, it assessed a number of variables at branch level to ensure that training could be tailored to individual needs. The thinking behind the approach was that individual branches may not have the skills and resources to develop an effective sales operation, so it was important to deal with them individually. A survey, which formed the basis of a training database, looked at each branch from a number of perspectives:

- size
- location and market coverage
- current skills and training record
- management structure
- customer profile.

The training organisation could develop tailored development programmes based on this information and the same information could also be used to plan other market development and support programmes.

Comparative size

Although it seems an obvious conclusion that larger branches can devote more resources to sales and marketing, the branch may not have the skills and resources to accomplish this. In looking at the training requirements of the branch, consider the number of people who are involved in marketing and customer service, the number of customers the branch deals with and their comparative turnover:

- Is the branch dealing with a small number of large customers or can it increase its customer base? Larger branches have the space to display more products and to devote more space to customer service.
- If they are members of a larger organisation, they will have the opportunity to use the facilities of the rest of the group and the head office and this can give them the ability to handle larger corporate clients.
- Smaller branches may not have the physical resources, but they can compensate by offering a flexible personal service to customers.
- Smaller branches may depend on larger local branches for their immediate marketing support and management – for example, a sub-branch might have only administrative staff and management and marketing may be handled from a larger local office; there would be difficulties in converting this branch to retailing.

Location

In assessing the potential contribution of the branch to the overall success of marketing operations, look at the location of the branch. Is it in the centre of a major conurbation, the catchment area for the business community or is it simply a local outlet with no clearly defined characteristics? The Speedwing Training survey looked at the location of branches to examine the type of business it might handle:

- If a branch was in a prime retail area it would attract a good level of passing trade. That meant merchandising, window displays and an attractive retail environment where people could browse would be important.
- Other branches which had lower passing trade depended on the quality of their telephone response and their ability to develop long-term relations with business customers where there was less emphasis on impulse purchasing and shopping around.

Skills

The change to a retailing culture demands entirely new skills in branch offices. Traditionally, branch office staff were content to offer their customers an efficient local service; staff who showed signs of ability would have been transferred to larger branches or, eventually, to head office, while the professional specialists would have been concentrated in head office or regional office teams to provide a central service.

Branches now have the responsibility of marketing their products and services aggressively and training and staff development should take account of this. The Speedwing survey asked local travel agents to provide details of the number of staff, their qualifications, experience and training record to date. These figures were compared with the forecast numbers and skills needed to run an effective sales and marketing operation in different size outlets. It was possible to develop a target branch skills profile and to identify the training needs for that branch.

Management structure

Management skills also need to be developed, managers have changing priorities in the new branch retailing environment; they need to gain competence in marketing, personal service, staff development and customer service as well as the inherent accounting and administrative skills. The management structure is likely to vary from branch to branch and could influence the success of the outlet. A branch where the senior manager is also the owner will have high motivation levels to achieve success and develop a level of service that meets customer needs. If the branch is large enough to support a management team, responsibility for marketing and for developing staff can be delegated.

The Speedwing survey looked at the management structure within travel agency branches to see how training could be used to improve local performance. They assessed:

- the manager's area of responsibility
- number of staff
- professional qualifications
- recent training record
- objectives
- customer service skills training
- retailing skills.

Using this information, they were able to develop targeted training programmes for individual managers and also to ensure that, through training, managers developed the flexibility to take on different roles within the agency network.

This improved career opportunities and helped to ensure consistent standards of service throughout the network.

Customer profile

Another important variation in corporate branch performance is customer profile. By identifying the type of customers each branch deals with, it is possible to fine-tune a training and support package to develop the right combination of skills. In the Speedwing Training survey, travel agencies were asked to identify the type of business, number of customers and frequency of purchase under a number of headings:

- business travel
- holiday travel
- scheduled or charter business
- special interest travel.

The principle of categorising customers can be applied to any type of business and used to develop a support programme.

USING THE RESEARCH INFORMATION

The information from the survey was used to develop a training communications programme:

- Individual travel agents were only sent information on standard courses that were relevant to their local needs.
- Speedwing were able to identify specific training needs that were not met by standard training programmes. They had the information to develop customised courses.
- The information and the communications programme enabled them to build long-term relationships with travel agents and meet their changing needs.

BENEFITS OF THE PROGRAMME

By working in partnership with Speedwing Training, the travel agents were able to improve their own business performance. Customisation enabled the travel agents to make better use of the training services that were available and concentrate their resources on improving individual business skills. Speedwing were able to provide the right level of support and build stronger relationships with travel agents to secure their loyalty. By developing a training service that focused on individual customer needs, they were able to demonstrate high levels of customer care.

KEY MANAGEMENT ACTIONS

- Identify opportunities for customising services.
- Assess the importance and potential customer service benefit of customisation.
- Assess the resource requirements for developing a customised service.
- Research the requirements of individual customers.
- Incorporate customer information in a database to support the customisation process.
- Review the customisation process with customers.

SUMMARY

This chapter explains the importance of customising support material and outlines the benefits to companies supplying both products and services. Using the example of local travel agents, it explains why individual outlets should be treated separately and provided with customised support packages, rather than uniform programmes. The chapter then explains how Speedwing Training researched the needs of individual travel agents as a basis for developing a training communications programme and customising their training services to the needs of individual branches.

Self-assessment checklist

- How important is the performance of local branches or distributors to your business success?

- What are the most important local support requirements?

- Can you meet support requirements through standard programmes?

- What do you need to know to develop customised programmes?

- Do you have the resources to develop customised programmes?

- Do you have sufficient customer information for customisation or do you need to carry out further research?

- Will customisation strengthen relations with your branches?

10

SIMPLIFYING CUSTOMERS' BUSINESS PROCESSES

This chapter describes a number of ways in which companies strengthen relationships with customers by simplifying the customers' business processes. The chapter includes the following examples:

- managing customers' energy processes
- joint market development
- supporting manufacturers with a logistics service
- reducing the impact on the balance sheet – partnership in fleet management
- using technology to build partnership with distributors in the travel industry.

MANAGING CUSTOMERS' ENERGY PROCESSES

When the regional electricity companies were privatised, they were given the opportunity to market their energy beyond the former regional boundaries. Large industrial users were now offered greater choice – they should have the freedom to source their energy from any supplier. Price was an important factor in the negotiations, but it was not the only consideration. The electricity companies wanted to build stronger links with these large customers so that they could offer them a wide-ranging solution which would reduce overall energy costs.

The key elements of the service were:

- energy consultancy to assess the customer's current use of energy and recommend actions to reduce overall costs. The consultancy covered the customer's processes and control systems as well as operating patterns
- process development where the customer and the energy supplier worked together to develop modified or new processes that would make the most effective use of energy
- energy management services where the energy supplier took over the management of the customer's various energy suppliers, reducing the administra-

tive burden and introducing higher standards of professional energy management which would help to reduce overall costs.

This form of partnership provides the energy supplier with an opportunity to control important customers and markets by building powerful business relationships. It can also reduce the importance of price negotiation by offering the customer a complete business solution. The customer benefits by getting access to professional services that may save money in the long term and by focusing on all areas of potential cost reduction.

JOINT MARKET DEVELOPMENT – CHEMICAL SUPPLIER AND INDUSTRIAL MANUFACTURER

BP Chemicals supply a wide range of petrochemical products, and wanted to strengthen its relationships with important manufacturing customers. The company was able to compete effectively on price, quality and delivery, but realised that its long-term future depended on close co-operation with customers. One of the company's products was polyethylene, used in the manufacture of products such as piping for water, gas and waste.

BP Chemicals realised that, to sell more of the intermediate material, it would have to help its manufacturing customers market their products to end-users. In other words, it must help piping manufacturers sell the benefits of polyethylene piping to local authorities, utilities and contractors. They also realised that they had to help manufacturers develop processes to design and manufacture using polyethylene. Partnership would therefore operate at a number of different levels:

- joint marketing initiatives to promote the benefits of polyethylene piping to end-users
- design and technical support to help the partners develop their own design skills and make the most effective use of polyethylene
- manufacturing consultancy to ensure that manufacturers can handle the material cost-effectively.

This type of partnership is important in developing markets where there may be a lack of awareness of the overall benefits of the new product. Partners co-operate to increase the size of the overall market. As the market matures, this process of education will be less important, but the continuing partnership will be based on the achievement of joint objectives.

SUPPORTING PARTNERS WITH A LOGISTICS SERVICE

Logistics is the business of moving products quickly, efficiently and economically. Efficient logistics helps companies eliminate wastage from the production chain because stock and goods in transit tie up capital. Distribution in the UK costs just 5 per cent of sales – in Germany it is 10 per cent, so effective distribution can make a major contribution to a partner's efficiency and costs. Logistics consultants working in partnership with manufacturers and other organisations who depend on efficient distribution provide advice on topics such as:

- calculating whether central or regional distribution would be more cost effective
- analysing distribution needs
- developing tailored logistics packages
- managing or providing fleets and warehouses or other contract distribution services.

Consultants in the logistics business believe 80 per cent of multinationals in the EC will restructure distribution practices in the next few years, because distribution not only affects cost of sales, but also has an impact on cost of fixed assets such as warehousing, general storage and transport fleets. Efficient distribution also affects the quality of customer service and a number of leading companies have been taking partnership initiatives to help improve their partners' business performance:

- Car manufacturer, Toyota, has concentrated its dealer spare parts operations at Magna Park – a dedicated distribution centre in the middle of the UK transport system. The move has cut delivery time for stock orders from three days to one day, helping their dealers to offer their customers a better service.
- Retailer Asda has been able to cut restocking operations from 20 vehicles per shop per day to five.
- Ford dealer, Perrys, works in partnership with other Ford dealers, offering them an overnight parts delivery service. The dealers can get parts to their wholesale customers more quickly and can complete their repairs quickly. This enables them to improve customer satisfaction without investing in large stocks.

The group which set up the Magna Park distribution centre understand the growing importance of efficient European distribution and are setting up partnership agreements with European companies to establish a network of similar distribution centres in other countries. The development is mirrored by the growth of larger groupings of transport companies to tackle problems on a European or global scale:

- UK haulage specialist, DFDS, who specialised in Anglo-Scandinavian trade has joined the TEAM-Alliance group of European transport firms
- Transport Development Group is planning a 2,500 European transport fleet
- Emery Worldwide invested in Warehouse Inventory System Express (WISE) programme which helps firms trying to establish a presence in a new market by solving initial launch and distribution problems
- Euroline, a consortium of European parcels carriers, will be using Belgium as a central hub to move products across Europe. The network covers 15 countries and offers customers a 36 to 72-hour service.

This type of partnership involves many different types of company including manufacturers, logistics consultancies, warehouse management groups and transport companies. It can take the form of partnership between distribution specialists and manufacturers, or between different distribution specialists to improve the quality of service available.

REDUCING THE IMPACT ON THE BALANCE SHEET – PARTNERSHIP IN FLEET MANAGEMENT

Operating a fleet of cars, vans or lorries imposes capital and operating costs and ties up valuable management time. In a bid to improve flexibility and retain control over their fleet operations, companies are now taking advantage of the growing number of partnership services available in this field.

Larger service or manufacturing companies with skills in managing their own fleets can offer this partnership service to other organisations. For example, Southern Water subsidiary, Topmark Vehicle Contracts, supply vehicles for any application, buy and lease back vehicles from companies to reduce their capital, or offer advice on selecting vehicles or operating a fleet.

Walon, a French company, and one of the top four distributors of cars from factories to dealerships and fleet owners, provides a managed vehicle distribution service for manufacturers. They provide a range of added value services and provide the manufacturer with complete control over their vehicles. They have also set up computer networks which can be linked to customers' networks to provide up-to-date management and control information. The company also works in partnership with car dealers helping them to improve the quality of customer service by providing a critical service like Pre-Delivery Inspection (PDI). They prepare new cars by dewaxing, cleaning, fitting special equipment such as telephones and badging them with company logos. PDI is a critical process in customer satisfaction and is handled by an organisation which has BS 5750.

PHH the supplier of All Star Cards provide fleet operators with fuel management services. The company issue charge cards to fleet operators so that drivers can pay for fuel without using cash, credit cards or accounts – all of which are costly to administer and open to abuse by drivers paying for other items. The All Star card is for fuel only and the fleet operators receive fully itemised records of all transactions, broken down in different ways to suit a company accounting system. PHH also supply management information to help the company analyse fuel costs as a proportion of operating costs. PHH can improve the partnership links further by providing electronic links with the fleet operator's own information systems to provide comprehensive up-to-date information.

Other card operators are helping fleet operators to improve and simplify fleet administration by adding other services to the basic fuel card. For example, a petrol company and a vehicle manufacturer were planning to work in partnership to deliver a combined fuel and service charge card. The fleet drivers would be able to have their vehicles repaired or serviced at any of the dealerships in the manufacturer's network and they would, of course, be able to buy their fuel at any of the oil company's outlets. The joint venture would provide a number of benefits for the partners and the fleet operators:

● The fleet operators would have a single source of management information, simplifying their own administrative processes and improving control.
● The fleet operators would be able to offer a better standard of service to their drivers by improving convenience.
● The car manufacturer would be able to offer a better package to fleet operators, helping to improve relationships and secure business.
● The car manufacturer would be able to secure higher levels of service business for the dealership network.
● The petrol company would be able to improve penetration of the fleet market by offering a combined fuel/service charge card which represented added value.

USING TECHNOLOGY TO BUILD PARTNERSHIP WITH DISTRIBUTORS IN THE TRAVEL INDUSTRY

Thomson Holidays used technology to build partnership with travel agents. The company installed a system called TOP (Thomson open-line programme) in travel agents to give them instant access to the company's holidays. These were the benefits:

- The system was popular with travel agents because it speeded up and cut the cost of enquiries and bookings, particularly at peak times.
- The system enabled Thomson to reduce labour-intensive booking costs, with a saving in the region of £28 million over a five-year period.
- It also enabled them to handle high levels of demand at peak periods, or when business increased, without taking on additional staff.
- They could also market aggressively knowing that they could handle the resulting demand.
- They forced their competitors to follow with similar systems, but they had already established the industry standard, and the high level of investment made the cost of entry prohibitively high for others.
- They deliberately left the system 'open' so that they could not be accused of bias or forcing travel agents to be locked in.

KEY MANAGEMENT ACTIONS

The chapter has described a number of examples of companies supporting their business customers by reducing the complexity and burden of internal tasks. The actions required to implement these programmes are wide-ranging and it is not practicable to cover them all. However, there are a number of general actions that can be taken to implement this type of strategy:

- Review your customers' business processes and assess whether you have the skills to help simplify or support those processes.
- Assess the importance of the process to the customer.
- Analyse the potential impact of the service on your business and your customers' business.
- Commit adequate resources to ensure service delivery is to the highest standards.

SUMMARY

This chapter has described a number of ways in which companies strengthen relationships with customers by simplifying the customers' business processes. Partnership can be used to differentiate products and services that are otherwise subject to stringent price negotiation. To support the launch of a new product or service that has a low level of awareness and understanding in the market-place, companies can undertake joint market development projects. Logistics is a key factor in reducing the overall cost of production and improving standards of customer service. Logistics partnership can help partners improve performance. Fleet management is an example of a specific partnership service that can help customers attack problems on the balance sheet or improve customer service. Technology can help to build effective relationships with distributors and improve local customer service by achieving higher levels of consistency.

Self assessment checklist

- Do you operate large contracts with major customers and are they subject to price negotiation?

- Could you use partnership to overcome price barriers?

- Can you utilise customer services to differentiate your product or service and build partnership?

- Do the customer services build long-term relationships?

- Do your customers need technical or manufacturing support to make use of the new products?

- How important are logistics to your partners' business performance?

- Can you offer them advice and guidance?

- Can you offer them physical resources to improve logistics performance or reduce costs?

- Can you enhance your own logistics capability through regional partnerships?

- Can you offer management or support services to help your customers improve their internal processes?

- Can you use technology to improve local marketing performance and control?

- Will technology enable you to improve customer service through distributor outlets?

11

CUSTOMER CONTACT STRATEGIES

This chapter explains the importance of regular communications with your customers. It stresses the importance of carrying out regular communications audits to see how well key decision makers understand you and describes a number of techniques for maintaining contact, including:

- direct marketing
- product updates
- technical/research updates
- customer team briefings on corporate progress
- corporate/financial information
- company direction
- customer satisfaction surveys
- customer performance review meetings
- customer account team manuals.

CARRYING OUT A COMMUNICATIONS AUDIT

This is an audit of the planned and current communications between an information systems company and its largest client. It is concerned with the relationship and image of the supplier from the customer's point of view. It compares the customer's views with those of the supplier and incorporates the customer's views of competitors. The audit compares the actual perceptions against current communications activities and highlights key communications actions needed to achieve the target perception.

Summary of audit

This is the management summary of the findings of the audit.

The company is setting out to improve the value, market share and quality of its business with this key account, increasing market share from 19 to 25 per cent. To achieve this, the company must secure strategic supplier status and enter a significant collaboration agreement with the customer.

Over the last year the company has improved its image within the key account, but competitors have made further gains. In certain areas the company is highly regarded, but research shows that the customer's senior managers are not aware of the company's current improvement programme. At worst, this means that the company may not be considered for certain major projects and, at best, the company may start at a disadvantage compared with its competitors. The company needs to develop a preference for its products and services, especially in the key areas identified for future business. A strong image development programme will be required to change the attitudes of the customer's senior management team.

This is a summary of the company's current image position:

- The company is almost as 'visible' as its competitors, but is only rated third in all issues associated with image.
- Contact with the customer at all levels is less than professional. According to the customer, the company does not understand its business and its products, and does not communicate its future strategies.
- There is a legacy of poor reputation which has largely been overcome by increased product reliability, but the image persists in the minds of the customer's senior management team.
- The company is perceived as offering lower quality and lower performance than competitors, and users are less satisfied than competitive users.
- The company is seen as losing ground with important decision makers.
- The company is identified more clearly than competitors with specific product lines, but is not rated most highly as the potential supplier of those products.
- The company's major weakness is perceived as its narrow product line and lack of expertise in certain areas.

From an image development point of view, there are three major actions needed to ensure future success:

- The reality of improved performance, reliability and value for money must be sustained and improved.
- The professionalism of the company's staff, their knowledge of their products and understanding of the customer's needs must be improved. The quality and effectiveness of all contacts with the customer must be improved dramatically.
- A positive, well-managed and consistent image development programme must be put in place to publicise the company's progress to close the gap

between perception and reality and to create a preference for the company by presenting the right messages to the right members of the management team.

Changing perceptions

The major perceptions which must be created to achieve the business goals are:

- The company is a professional organisation which understands the customer's business needs and can meet them with a wide range of high quality products and services.
- The company is technically successful in major projects, developing total solutions and delivering value for money, on time, every time;
- The company is winning market share from its competitors.
- The company is an approved and respected strategic supplier with whom it is safe to place business.
- The company is a successful and financially stable company with a sound management team – a good prospective supplier and business partner.

Communicating professionalism

'The company is a professional organisation which understands the customer's business needs and can meet them with a wide range of high quality products and services.' The messages to support this perception include:

- The company is investing £** in training over the next year.
- The company is organised into market-focused groups to offer the highest standards of service.
- *** staff are dedicated to the customer's business.
- The company is committed to total quality.
- The company has developed a broad product range and a full range of support services.
- The company's products meet international standards.
- The new product development programme is providing innovative new products.

Communicating technical success

'The company is technically successful in major projects, developing total solutions and delivering value for money, on time, every time.' The important messages to support this perception include:

- The company has an established reputation for innovation.
- The company's products have been selected for the following demanding applications . . .
- Customers are saving money by using the company's products.
- The company's products conform to international standards.
- The company has a research and development budget in excess of £*** and has a team of *** highly skilled people dedicated to technical support.

Communicating market success

'The company is winning market share from its competitors.' The important messages to support this perception include:

- The company has been selected to provide products and services to the following customers . . .
- The company has recently won a major order worth £**.
- The company has been selected as a strategic supplier to the following customers . . .
- The company has gained ** per cent market share in the last year, while competitors have lost ** per cent share in the last year.

Communicating strategic supplier status

'The company is an approved and respected strategic supplier with whom it is safe to place business.' The important messages to support this perception include:

- The company has been selected as a strategic supplier to the following market-leading customers . . .
- The company is collaborating with a major international organisation.
- The company meets the following international product and quality standards.

Communicating corporate stability

'The company is successful and financially stable and has a sound management team – a good prospective supplier and business partner.' The important messages to support this perception include:

- The company's annual results show ** per cent growth in orders, revenue and profits.

- The company is expanding.
- The company is a member of the *** international group.
- The company is the leading European supplier.

The audit has identified the key areas for improving communications performance and it is essential that these messages should be communicated consistently in every form of contact with the customer.

COMMUNICATIONS STRATEGY

The remainder of this chapter looks at different techniques for communicating with the customer.

Direct marketing

Direct marketing is used to send targeted communications to named individuals. On a key account, these might be important members of the decision-making team who cannot be contacted directly or who require specific information. Direct marketing can take the form of direct mail letters, brochures, management guides or other publications that meet the reader's main concerns. Direct marketing can also be used to make special promotional offers to named individuals – invitations to seminars, offers of reprints of technical articles, free copies of business briefing guides and other items that enhance your credibility as a supplier. A direct marketing programme is based on planned, regular communications to ensure that each decision maker holds a favourable perception of your company. A programme targeting the technical director aims to position the company as an innovative, technically advanced supplier. The programme might include:

- reprints of published articles by technical specialists on your staff
- a briefing and update on your latest research programme
- an independent review of your product performance
- invitations to a seminar sponsored by your company on industry developments.

By looking at the information requirements of the key decision makers, you can develop a comprehensive direct marketing programme.

Product updates

It is vital that your customers' technical and purchasing specialists always have the latest information on your products. This is not only sound engineering practice, it alerts them to any new developments that may help them to develop their own products. You can use a formal system of change control to ensure that each of your contacts is kept up to date.

Technical/research updates

These are similar to product updates, but they notify your customers of future developments so that they can incorporate new technology into their own forward programmes. This type of update not only enhances your technical reputation, it helps to build closer working relationships between the technical groups. These updates can be published occasionally or at regular intervals, say quarterly or annually.

Customer team briefings on corporate progress

Significant developments such as new investment programmes, acquisitions, changes in management, expansion programmes or new product launches are of major interest to your key account customers. By bringing together the two teams, you can take the opportunity to update everyone of the progress and ensure that there are experts on hand to deal with specific issues.

Corporate/financial information

Although financial information is an integral element of the team-briefing process, you can keep individual decision makers up to date by sending copies of corporate brochures, financial results and other corporate information. A regular flow of information will ensure that key influencers are aware of your financial performance and remain confident of your ability as a stable supplier.

Company direction

It is important that your key customers understand the future direction of your company – how you see your business in the medium and long term, what new developments you plan to introduce, and whether you are considering any fundamental changes to your business. They need to be convinced that you will remain committed to the success of their business and that they will continue to benefit from working closely with you. An understanding of your future direction helps your customers plan their own development.

Customer satisfaction surveys

As well as keeping customers informed of developments in your company, it is also important to monitor their attitudes to your company and your performance on their account. Customer satisfaction surveys are covered in more detail later in the book, but they should be an integral element of a two-way communications strategy.

Customer performance review meetings

As well as measuring customer satisfaction, you should be prepared to review your performance with your key customers and discuss measures for improving performance. By taking a proactive attitude to performance measurement, you demonstrate high levels of customer care and improve relationships with team members. Review meetings can be held at a number of different levels:

- monthly progress meetings on technical and commercial matters, involving specialist members of the team
- quarterly review meetings on overall performance. Most of the team will participate and the meeting will be used to identify any remedial actions needed
- annual reviews involving senior members of the team to review performance and discuss key objectives for the coming year.

Customer account team manuals

In a key account environment where a large number of people are involved, an account team manual can be extremely useful. The manual should include all the information needed to operate the account, and would be distributed to members of both teams. The contents of the manual might include:

- introductory section on the general benefits of working together, focusing on the opportunities to improve business performance and maintain a competitive edge
- the key performance measurements used to assess progress
- the scope of the account relationship, including supply and distribution arrangements, action programmes and levels of technical and marketing co-operation
- an outline of the direction in which the account could develop, including a growth path and possible action programmes
- the quality processes and feedback mechanisms that would be used to control the programme

- the skills and resources of both companies
- the organisation of the two companies, including appropriate personnel details
- the responsibilities of both parties and the reporting procedures
- contact information explaining the communications links between the two companies and the sources of information within each
- escalation procedures to deal with any problems on the account
- a summary of the main benefits and long-term objectives of the account relationship.

A manual is a valuable technique for building understanding and maintaining relationships between the two parties. It ensures that everyone understands their role and shows how the relationship can be utilised to provide benefits for both parties.

SUMMARY

Regular communication with decision makers is essential to the success of customer focus. However, the communications programme must be based on carefully researched information needs. A communications audit can help you to assess attitudes towards your company and provides the basis for planning a communications strategy. Direct marketing can be used to ensure that individual decision makers receive the information they need, while product and technical updates ensure that your customers are kept fully informed on your technical performance. Regular briefings on corporate and financial developments build confidence and ensure that your company is regarded as a stable supplier. It is also important to assess customer attitudes to your performance and discuss improvement programmes through a series of regular team progress meetings. Large account teams can become unwieldy, but an account team manual will help to keep both parties informed about each other.

Self-assessment checklist

Can you audit your key customer's understanding of your business?

- Who would be the most important contacts?

- What image do you want your customers to hold of you?

- How much do you have to change customer perceptions to establish yourself as a preferred supplier?

- What is the key information to be communicated to your customers?

- Which decision makers are most difficult to reach and how could you use direct marketing to contact them regularly?

- Do you have an established technical and product update programme?

- Which decision makers should you contact with corporate and financial information?

- Do you have a formal method of measuring customer satisfaction and do you review the results with your customers?

- What information should you include in an account team manual?

12

COURTESY SERVICES

According to motor manufacturers, inconvenience is the biggest single factor mentioned by customers when asked about their views on service. When a car is off the road, the consumer has to find alternative means of transport or make separate arrangements for carrying out tasks that involve transport. When motorists were asked how they would like service improved, a high percentage indicated that anything that reduced the inconvenience would be welcome – low-price hire cars, free transport to and from a destination or the use of a replacement car came high on the list of priorities. Customers also indicated that, if they had to choose from a number of alternative suppliers, they would choose the one that offered the least inconvenience and they would continue to use that outlet provided it maintained the same levels of convenience.

This is the background to a change that has now been adopted by many of the major motor manufacturers – providing a courtesy car or an alternative form of transport when customers bring their cars in for service or repair. The concept of a courtesy car is not only proving a powerful method of winning service business, it is an important factor in retaining customer loyalty provided the programme is used effectively.

APPLYING THE COURTESY CAR PRINCIPLE

The same principle of reducing inconvenience can be applied to other types of business:

- office equipment manufacturers who offer a repair service off-site, providing replacement equipment during the repair
- domestic electrical equipment during off-site repairs
- on a larger scale, disaster recovery specialists, providing temporary accommodation and computer systems for customers who have lost their premises and computer systems because of fire or some other disaster
- recruitment consultants who offer temporary staff at all levels on a project basis for short- and medium-term requirements.

Courtesy services can prove to be an important factor in the following business scenarios:

- when product service or repair causes inconvenience to the customer. The degree of inconvenience varies – a doctor or sales representative, for example, would suffer a great deal of inconvenience while their car was off the road, while someone who simply used the car to travel to and from work would suffer minor inconvenience if there was no alternative transport;
- when loss of the product or service for maintenance or repair affects the customer's business directly. The loss of a computer system, for example, would be devastating to a company that relied on computers to offer a service such as Automatic Teller Machines, or operate equipment such as Computer Numerically-Controlled manufacturing systems, while the loss of a computer to a company that used them for administrative tasks such as accounting or management reporting would be inconvenient, but not disastrous;
- when a company offers a service that could be easily duplicated with an opportunity to differentiate the service by improving convenience;
- when a company wants to improve long-term customer loyalty by developing a service strategy that builds in high levels of customer convenience. The company recognises that a product/service package is not sufficient, the solution must help the customer to run their business efficiently with minimum inconvenience. The service strategy therefore includes replacement and convenience elements focused on the customers' business needs;
- customers purchase a routine service product regularly and there is an opportunity to reward their loyalty. Courtesy cars, for example, can be used in a selective way to reward customer loyalty and act as an additional incentive to continue purchase;
- when a company wishes to demonstrate its customer focus and increase the level of satisfaction. Courtesy services are shown by research to have high levels of customer interest and can therefore be a powerful factor in customer satisfaction.

PROGRAMME OBJECTIVES

When the car manufacturers introduced courtesy car services, they set the following business objectives:

- to increase customer satisfaction and loyalty over the whole ownership period so that the customer would repurchase from the manufacturer when they bought their next car. This objective was vital because the customer's experience of a car was not just tied to product performance and reliability, but on the cost and convenience of ownership. Customer satisfaction was therefore vital at every stage of ownership;

- to win back service business from independent service outlets; the dealer network was perceived as expensive and inconvenient compared with independent outlets such as Halfords or other groups which offered modular services at value for money prices with no bookings necessary and concentrated on the more popular forms of service such as exhausts, tyres, brakes and interim services. The franchised group wanted to demonstrate that they could offer the same level of convenience with the bonus that they were offering manufacturers' standards of service. A courtesy car service would therefore prove a vital element in winning back the business;

- to maintain service and loyalty; as well as winning service business, they also had to retain it. The courtesy car programme was a bonus in both senses; by offering it regularly to important customers who needed the convenience, they retain their loyalty and by offering the courtesy car as an occasional bonus to regular service customers they could reward loyalty;

- to promote the dealer network with a powerful argument to build customer loyalty; this objective is important for companies that depend on the effective performance of a dealer network. The courtesy car programme can ensure that dealers provide the right levels of care to their customers and build the long-term customer loyalty that is essential to the sale of future products.

OPERATING THE PROGRAMME

Operating a programme like courtesy car is a relatively simple concept but the administrative requirements are considerable and could prove cumbersome if they are not handled effectively. The basis of the programme is that a courtesy car is offered to service or repair customers who would suffer inconvenience if their car is not available. Because of the high volume of such customers going through each dealership, it is not possible to offer a courtesy car to every customer so the offer has to be discretionary. Manufacturers offer guidelines on identifying prospective courtesy car users:

- customers whose car is essential to their work such as doctors, nurses, sales representatives or business customers
- high profile customers who are regarded as opinion formers – journalists, local government officials, fleet owners, business people

- customers whose cars are in for repairs that are likely to take more than a day on the basis that they would suffer considerable inconvenience
- regular service customers as a reward for their loyalty
- drivers with young children on the basis that public transport could prove to be a problem.

The guidelines include a sensible combination of customer care and targeted marketing, but they demonstrate the importance of controlling the programme carefully at local level and tailoring the programme to local market conditions. The discretionary nature of the courtesy car programme means that the local distributor must have other options for reducing inconvenience for other customers. The programme would have limited value if it was seen as élitist. The other services include:

- courtesy bus taking customers to their destinations in the morning
- collection and delivery service to the customer's home or business processes
- low-cost car hire services
- agreements with public transport operators to provide complimentary or low-cost services for customers. Although the techniques may be different the customers benefit in the same way from reduced inconvenience and the distributor should ideally offer a balanced portfolio of courtesy services.

The choice of courtesy cars is an important part of the process. It would be easy for the dealer to have a couple of old runarounds for occasional use by customers. However, the service had to reflect the quality of the customer product. Most manufacturers insist that their distributors operate a special courtesy car fleet which meets specific requirements:

- The cars are the latest models available.
- They are less than a year old.
- The maximum mileage is specified.
- The fleet contains a mix of models to reflect the overall range.
- The cars are regularly serviced.
- Each car is inspected between users so that it operates reliably.

Provided the cars meet those conditions, they are allowed to remain on the courtesy car fleet, but as soon as their age or mileage falls outside the programme limits, they are taken off the fleet and can be marketed through the manufacturers' used car programmes. The aim of the fleet is to ensure that the customer has an opportunity to sample different products in the range and sees the cars at their best.

To help the dealer buy and operate a courtesy car fleet, manufacturers offer a number of financial incentives and support packages. Dealers are offered low-cost finance schemes to purchase the fleet cars and residual values are often maintained at a higher level to encourage dealers to replace their fleet cars at regular intervals. Dealers are also given a series of rebates related to levels of courtesy car usage.

The rebates are intended to offset the management and operating costs of the programme and also to ensure that the courtesy cars are given to the maximum number of customers to ensure widespread cost benefits. Early courtesy car schemes suffered from cumbersome rebate procedures which many dealers found difficult to operate:

● Rebates were calculated on units of usage.
● A morning or afternoon was a unit with an overnight usage counting as a further unit.
● Complex formulae were used to calculate the unit value of loans where customers had to wait longer for a repair to be completed or returned their vehicle later.
● Reduced rebates were paid on cars that were out for long-term loans where the customer was having extensive repairs carried out or where there was a delay because products were not available.

This approach worked to a degree but it proved difficult because of disagreements about how long a loan period should be calculated. Later programmes were simplified to concentrate on the number of customers who used the vehicles. This helped the programme to meet its original objective of reducing inconvenience for the greatest number of customers and simplified administration for the dealer.

Administration for the customer was also reduced to a minimum to ensure that the offer of a courtesy car did not prove to be a burden. The only information required from a customer was a current driving license and proof of age. Courtesy cars were not given to young drivers and the car manufacturer arranged special insurance cover for courtesy car drivers. The driver's only requirements were to return the car in the condition in which it left the dealership, i.e. with no accident damage and with nothing missing and to pay for petrol that was used. The loan agreement was made deliberately simple so that the customer collected the courtesy car with the minimum of fuss.

A programme such as courtesy car provided strong benefits for customers, dealers and manufacturers but it involved a considerable degree of administration which could have put a drain on a manufacturer's resources. It was essential that the programme was managed centrally to ensure consistently high standards across the dealer network and to ensure that the dealership would operate the programme effectively. Many manufacturers set up external administrative agencies to handle this aspect for them.

BENEFITS OF THE PROGRAMME

Courtesy car programmes have helped manufacturers to reduce levels of inconvenience to their customers and increase overall customer satisfaction. Increased satisfaction means that customers are likely to return to the manufacturer and the dealership when they are considering their next car purchase. The courtesy car programme also allows dealers and manufacturers to selectively reward their most loyal customers and that can also contribute to customer satisfaction. By offering customers a service that research showed was very important, both manufacturers and distributors were able to improve their competitive position.

KEY MANAGEMENT ACTIONS

- Research the importance of courtesy services to customers.
- Identify the key customers who should be offered the service.
- Offer other courtesy options to customers who do not qualify for the full service.
- Ensure that the replacement product is a quality, reliable product that conveys the right image of the company.
- Set guidelines on the age and condition of replacement products.
- Provide financial support to encourage local outlets to participate in the programme.
- Simplify programme administration for both consumer and local outlet.

SUMMARY

The use of courtesy services such as courtesy cars is helping companies to increase customer satisfaction by reducing inconvenience for customers. The principle can also be applied to other sectors where customers can be inconvenienced when a product is under repair. A courtesy programme should be simple to administer for both customer and manufacturer and should demonstrate high levels of customer care.

Self-assessment checklist

- Do service and repairs cause inconvenience for your customers?
- How could that inconvenience be reduced?

- Do levels of inconvenience vary by customer?

- Can you offer customers a range of options to reduce inconvenience?

- What resources would be required to operate a courtesy programme?

- What standards should be applied to the courtesy product?

- What would the programme administrative requirements be?

- Can you offer consistent programme standards throughout a network?

13

CARING FOR CUSTOMERS DURING AN INCIDENT

The chapter on courtesy services showed how important it is to reduce inconvenience for customers. Customers who can relax knowing that their problems are taken care of will be fully satisfied with the services that are available and will be happy to deal with the same outlet in the future. Research into service standards indicated that reassurance was one of the prime considerations. Psychologists working with quality experts found out that a key factor in delivering time-guaranteed services was the ability to reassure customers that help was on the way. Customers would then be prepared to wait until help or support arrived even if there was a long gap between reporting the incident and having it resolved.

So, if vital manufacturing equipment broke down, the equipment supplier would offer a 24-hour, 4-hour or 1-hour call out service. Customers, as research showed, were not too concerned how long the repair would take provided they were kept informed. Attitudes like this are valuable in forming customer response strategies – how long should a service call take, what level of cover should be provided, how should support requests be handled, what happens if the incident is not resolved within an agreed time-scale?

Questions like these are essential to the efficient handling of customer problems. This chapter looks at different ways of dealing with customer problems and uses the example of the motoring services Personal Incident Manager to illustrate one approach to problem management. The Personal Incident Manager approach is to appoint one person, trained in customer service skills to deal with a customer throughout an incident – reassuring the customer, providing advice and guidance, co-ordinating the support services and keeping the customer informed on progress.

WHEN THE APPROACH IS USEFUL

The same principles can be applied to any service-led organisation where the customer needs to be kept informed – maintenance and support services on vital equipment for example, or disaster recovery services where the customer faces many difficult and unfamiliar decisions and needs constant support to reassure them. Companies who provide travellers cheques offer their customers a 24-hour helpline anywhere in the world to get financial help or advice on their holiday money. Lost cheques or exchange problems can be handled efficiently with minimum disruption to the holiday giving the customer peace of mind and increasing customer satisfaction.

Insurance companies offer their customers helplines for motoring cases or domestic problems. The customer can call, get immediate support services, plus advice on how to proceed and make a claim. The same principle of re-assurance applies. During an incident, the customer can be uncertain of how to proceed and welcomes advice and guidance to minimise distress and inconvenience.

A number of scenarios can be used to identify situations where support like this could be valuable:

- The customer could suffer a great deal of inconvenience and stress as a result of the incident – reducing the stress and inconvenience would help to demonstrate high levels of care and increase customer satisfaction.
- The incident could threaten the efficiency of the company business and measures must be taken to limit the damage.
- The customer does not have the skills and resources to resolve the problems on the spot and is dependent on external forms of support.
- The customer has paid for a support package and has agreed to a certain level of response. The company must respond within the agreed levels.
- The speed of response is seen as a competitive differentiator and is positioned as an integral part of the service package.
- Failure to deal with the incident quickly could have a critical effect on the customer's business or personal activities.
- The incident could have legal implications and the customer needs high levels of advice and guidance.

PROGRAMME OBJECTIVES

In developing a response and support strategy, a company sets a wide range of business objectives:

- to provide the highest levels of customer support during an incident
- to minimise inconvenience for the customer
- to ensure that incidents are resolved promptly within agreed time-scales
- to provide customers with quality response and support throughout an inci-

dent

- to ensure that support resources are deployed effectively to maximise customer satisfaction.

OPERATING THE PROGRAMME

The Personal Incident Manager approach is used as part of a number of motoring packages offered by the RAC. The packages are grouped together under the heading 'assured mobility' and are offered direct to private motorists, branded as a fleet service or part of a car manufacturer's drivers' package. The overall package includes the following elements:

- roadside, home and rescue services for simple repairs
- recovery of the vehicle to the customer's next destination or home
- alternative methods of onward transport for the customer, including contribution to the cost of public transport, hire car or hotel costs for overnight accommodation.

The role of the Personal Incident Manager is to take responsibility for the provision of these services and to reassure the customer that help and support are on the way. The Personal Incident Manager:

- takes the incoming calls from the customer, establishes location and identifies the form of support needed
- provides individual guidance to the customer on action to be taken with an indication of the support that will be provided
- deals with the customers' immediate queries
- makes detailed arrangements to put support services into operation, makes hotel, car hire or hotel bookings on behalf of the customer and arrange settlement
- informs family or business colleagues on the customer's behalf
- monitors progress on the support services and keep the customer up to date if possible. Many telephone companies are now 'bundling' vehicle rescue services with mobile phones to ensure that a customer can be kept up to date during an incident.

The support service compares favourably with all the problems a customer might face if he or she had to co-ordinate all the support activities themselves – contacting a rescue organisation, finding a repair centre, booking a hotel, getting to the next destination or home by public transport while being in a state of distress after a breakdown or accident. The Personal Incident Manager approach aims to reduce the 'hassle' in an incident and allows the customers to get on with their normal business.

Many of the leading computer manufacturers use similar techniques to support their customers after a disaster – fire, accident, system breakdown or some other serious incident. If the customer loses the computer system for an extended period, this could seriously threaten the future of the business. Research showed that only a minority of companies that claimed to depend on the computer had a formal disaster recovery strategy, and the research also pointed out that loss of a system for more than a few days could effectively put them out of business.

The disaster recovery programme has a number of stages:

- consultancy to help the customer identify critical activities that should be covered in the event of a disaster
- training to help customer staff and managers prepare for a disaster by simulating the conditions of an emergency
- preparation of a contingency plan
- provision of replacement equipment and services in the event of an incident
- support and project management resources during an incident
- full support to restore normal service.

Throughout an incident, the customer would have access to an incident manager who would co-ordinate rescue and recovery activities and provide advice, guidance and support. The principle is similar to the Personal Incident Manager where customers are given reassurance that incidents will be resolved and they are sure of the highest standards of support throughout the incident.

BENEFITS OF THE PROGRAMME

A programme such as this enables a company to deliver the highest standards of customer care at a time when the customer most needs it. The service will therefore reinforce the relationship with the customer and ensure the highest levels of customer satisfaction. This level of support can help to differentiate a service from a competitive product by offering added value and the assurance of peace of mind.

IMPLEMENTING THE PROGRAMME

The programme has two main elements – the infrastructure to deliver the service and the personal skills to provide the right level of customer care. The infrastructure requires a significant investment to ensure that the service can be delivered rapidly and efficiently throughout the country. Depending on the complexity of the project, it might include:

- communications to provide a rapid response to customer queries and put the service into operation
- a trained support team to deliver the service
- quality-controlled suppliers to support the direct response team
- a control centre to manage the operations and co-ordinate the response
- a network of contacts and suppliers to provide the specialist services that form part of the response.

Skilled staff are essential to the effective delivery of the service. The skills requirements would include:

- incident management skills to deal with customers who may be in stressful situations
- project management skills to co-ordinate and implement a response
- technical skills to deliver the service
- communications skills to co-ordinate the elements of the programme.

SUMMARY

Incident management provides an opportunity to demonstrate the highest levels of customer care. Research shows that customers are less concerned with the time taken to deliver a response, and more concerned with receiving reassurance that their problems are being resolved. Operations like the RAC Personal Incident Manager or disaster recovery services show that personal care can be delivered on a national scale and can embrace complex scenarios. Considerable infrastructure and communications resources are required to deliver a consistent standard of service round the clock, but the investment in this level of service can result in high levels of customer satisfaction.

Self-assessment checklist

- What types of incident are your customers likely to face?
- What would the personal or business impact of the incident be?
- How can you help your customers to prepare for an incident?
- How could you provide support to help them overcome problems faced by the incident?

- What are the resource and investment implications of a support service?
- Could you deliver the support services yourself or would you need to co-ordinate the activities of third party specialists?
- Do your staff have the skills to deliver the different elements of the service?

14

USING TECHNOLOGY TO IMPROVE CUSTOMER SERVICE

Technology can be used to improve the quality of customer service by making it easier for companies to respond to customer requests. A call reception centre, for example, which co-ordinates all the incoming service calls enables a company to manage the quality of its telephone response. Technology alone cannot improve the quality of service, technology plus the right equipment is a powerful combination.

The ICL Connection is a good example of a call response strategy which makes full use of the power of technology to deliver service. The Connection uses telecommunications technology to link customers anywhere in the UK with specialists anywhere in the UK and represents a major investment in training and technology. The Connection is an example of a major investment in high technology and training, but companies can obtain the same benefits on a smaller scale:

- Providing customers with a round-the-clock response service may be sufficient to maintain high levels of customer loyalty. A helpline reassures customers that they have the full support and backing of a professional organisation.
- Using technology to provide customers with a diagnostic and monitoring service provides round-the-clock peace of mind that their equipment is in secure hands. Security companies, for example, provide remote control centres that monitor the status of their customers' security systems and take immediate action to deal with faults or incidents.
- Service databases which retain comprehensive service and fault information on all a customer's equipment and installations enables a company to quickly interpret service requests and provide a rapid response.
- Software that provides help to individual equipment users can help customers to deal with routine maintenance and simple faults quickly without having to make service requests.

These examples of technology are now in common use, but companies

have assessed them from the point of view of service performance, rather than customer service benefits. The key benefit is reassurance and a quality response to customer service requirements.

WHEN THIS APPROACH IS SUITABLE

There are a number of scenarios where technology can be used to make a contribution to customer service.

Reliable equipment operation

Customers depend on the continual reliable operation of their equipment to maintain their competitive business performance; a rapid, quality response to service requests is vital; a bank cash-dispensing system must be constantly available and any faults dealt with quickly. Technology ensures that customers are able to operate their own business efficiently and deliver high standards of service to their own customers.

Consistent local service

A large customer base spread over a wide geographical territory and dealing with a company through a network of local branches expects consistent standards of service; if the company does not have the resources to offer the same level of service in each branch, it must find a way of centralising and allocating its resources so that customers can be offered that consistency.

Critical requests

Customers expect an immediate response to critical requests; motoring organisations, for example, know that customers who have broken down need reassurance and accurate information on the support they will receive. The motoring organisations have invested in communications technology that enables them to accurately pinpoint the location of breakdowns and respond quickly with help; response like this builds high levels of customer satisfaction by improving convenience.

Fault prevention

The technology exists to monitor equipment condition and predict service requirements before faults occur; companies supplying high value equipment can take advantage of sophisticated monitoring equipment to improve performance and reliability. Customers get a better return on their investment.

Product differentiation

Product differential is low, but quality and speed of service is a crucial factor in winning and maintaining business; the service package is proving to be a crucial factor in a customer's assessment of competitive offerings. Technology can be an important differentiator here. Innovative technology or technology that requires a major investment can create entry barriers for competitors and provide a valuable edge; the customer has identified service as the crucial factor.

Better account control

The company wants to improve account control; technological links not only provide the customer with higher standards of customer service, they help to strengthen relationships with the customer and prevent competitors from making inroads.

Service staff rely on information

The more a company knows about its customers, the better the standard of service it can deliver; customer databases can be invaluable in helping customer service staff quickly provide advice and guidance to customers over the phone. A service operation, for example, should hold complete service records of all customers' equipment, together with customer information. Any customer request can be quickly compared with information on the database as a basis for a prompt response.

SETTING PROGRAMME OBJECTIVES

These scenarios are important in both manufacturing and service businesses and they help companies to meet the following business objectives:

- Provide a rapid quality response to customer requests.
- Ensure that customers' equipment continues to operate reliably.
- Provide consistent standards of service across a network.
- Strengthen links with customers.
- Reinforce the benefits of quality personal service.

- Provide service staff with the support to deliver increasingly higher standards of service.

IMPLEMENTING THE PROGRAMME

Many of these objectives were important to ICL when they developed their customer response strategy. The company supplies mainframe and departmental computers to customers throughout Europe and provides them with a full range of support services from initial consultancy through to maintenance. Services are important to customers because they ensure that their equipment continues to operate reliably and provide business benefit.

To provide a national service to their customers throughout the UK, ICL had a network of local branches, each providing service to a defined group of customers. As in most branch networks, the larger branches had greater resources to provide service which meant that there was inconsistency throughout the network. At the same time it was critical for ICL and other computer manufacturers to maintain and build their service revenues. With declining equipment sales, the growth opportunities were in customer services. However, there was also an increasing number of competitors, particularly independent maintenance companies who were trying to win business on a combination of price and service.

Any erosion of the customer service base was bound to have an impact on long-term customer loyalty, so it was important to win and retain service business. The key to success for ICL was a combination of technology and customer care.

Technology would enable them to offer a more sophisticated service that was consistent across their customer base, but this had to be balanced with high standards of personal service from all staff so that the customers received the highest levels of care. The telephone is a good example of this dual approach. A company could invest large sums of money in a sophisticated telecommunications system, but if the calls were answered slowly or if the receptionist was unable to deal with the caller's request effectively, the investment in technology was effectively wasted.

There were a number of important aspects to the customer response strategy:

- centralisation of customer response through a national call reception centre which replaced calls to local branches;
- development of a customer response service which was monitored to independent quality standards;
- the introduction of centres of excellence for fault diagnosis and customer

support, providing consistent support to customers nationwide;

- the use of a sophisticated service database which maintained customer equipment information and provided comprehensive fault diagnosis information;
- the introduction of communications systems for field engineers that enabled them to access the database for support when they were working on the customer's site;
- the development of sophisticated monitoring systems which enabled ICL to manage the service of major installations more efficiently;
- the implementation of a company-wide customer care training programme which ensured that all staff were customer focused;
- the redeployment of branch service staff from direct service delivery and management to pro-active customer service roles;
- the development of partnership programmes with customers to make them aware of the importance of customer service and to ensure that they were able to take full advantage of ICL's new service programmes.

National call reception centre

The Connection was the name given to ICL's purpose-built call reception centre. Instead of dialling local branch numbers and obtaining local service, the customer could now dial a single number and have immediate access to any specialist within ICL. The calls were routed over the network and charged to the customers at local rates so that there was no cost penalty for using the new national service.

The Connection was available 24 hours a day throughout the year and was designed from the outset as a single reference point for all customer requests. Customers could report faults, request service visits, ask for telephone advice and guidance, request literature or register a complaint. Offering a single point of contact simplified the process of obtaining information or support and got round the problem of asking the customer to phone another extension or another number.

In many cases, the call receptionist was able to deal with the customer call immediately – logging a request, dealing with a query or providing information. However, where the call required the support of specialists, the receptionist took details of the call and co-ordinated the call-back process. The call receptionist would route the call to the appropriate specialist and then call back the customer to advise on the way the request would be handled. The call receptionist would then monitor progress on the response and keep the customer up to date with progress. The result – the customer was kept fully informed and had access to the most appropriate specialists.

Independent quality control

To ensure that customers received the highest standards of service, the operations of the call reception centre were subject to independent assessment by the British Standards Institution. Centre staff had to conform to a set of procedures under BS 5750 which monitored such features as:

- time to reply
- time to respond to the customer's request
- the call-back sequence
- the methods of logging calls and reviewing performance.

This ensured that customers could expect a consistent standard of response from the call reception centre.

Centres of excellence

The key to providing a consistent standard of service was the introduction of centres of excellence. Here product and technical specialists were concentrated in groups able to provide a high standard of service to all customers. The diagnostics centre, for example, dealt with fault reports. The customer report was passed by the call reception centre and the specialists were able to carry out further diagnosis over the telephone or work with an engineer on site by providing telephone support. The approach did not replace the traditional engineers on site; it simply made them more effective and freed them for more productive staff. It also overcame the resource problem of not having enough specialists to go round all the branches.

The other important task of the centres was to identify and co-ordinate the skills and parts that would be required to deal with reported faults. In diagnosing the customer fault by telephone, they were able to identify the type of engineer most appropriate for dealing with the fault and order the spares that would be required to complete the job. When engineers arrived on site, they would be fully equipped to complete the task without the frustrating experience of making multiple visits because parts were not available.

Service database

The service database was an integral part of the centres of excellence. ICL was able to collate worldwide information on the performance of its systems and to build up profiles of the faults and queries that were most frequent. This provided a number of important benefits:

- It allowed the specialists to provide a rapid response to routine service queries by comparing symptoms with the information on the database.

- It allowed ICL to identify the most common service requests and to provide information to customers which would eventually reduce the number of routine requests.
- It enabled ICL to develop customer support software that would allow customers to deal with simple service requirements themselves.
- The database also helped call receptionists and support specialists to gather preliminary detailed information on the customer's equipment and service history without wasting the customer's time answering routine questions.

Communications for site engineers

The database was also a valuable form of support for engineers working on customer sites. They were provided with specially-developed hand-held terminals which provided them with two-way access to the service database. The engineers were able to obtain diagnostic information which enabled them to complete the task quickly and they were also able to update the customer's service records immediately. The customer could feel confident that work would be carried out efficiently to the highest standards.

Monitoring systems

Although The Connection was designed to speed up the process of response to customer service requests, ICL also wanted to reduce the level of faults and service requests. This would not only demonstrate that their equipment was more reliable, it would simplify and reduce the customer's own service administration. Larger computer installations were therefore fitted with integral monitoring systems. These systems monitored the condition of critical components; if a component developed fault symptoms, the system alerted ICL service staff to take appropriate action. In that way, potential faults could be resolved before they caused problems for the customer.

Customer care training

As we said earlier, this investment in technology could have been wasted without a personal commitment to customer care on the part of every employee. Over the period of a year, ICL put all their staff through an intensive quality and customer care training programme. The training was backed by a range of corporate and personal quality initiatives that helped to develop a culture for constant improvement. Each individual was asked to analyse their own tasks and asked to assess how they might improve their working methods to meet customer needs more successfully.

Redeployment of branch staff

The changes in support procedures meant that branch staff now had less responsibility for service delivery. The customer no longer contacted a local branch, but a national call reception centre; service was delivered from national centres of excellence or by engineers who might not be located in the local branch. Although this reduced the routine service administration tasks, it also freed branch staff to be more pro-active and make customer care visits to customer care sites. This made their role more responsive than reactive and enabled them to play a wider role in delivering customer service.

Developing partnership

As part of the customer focus process, ICL implemented a partnership programme to help customers benefit from the new service developments. A Care and Support manual explained how services could help customers improve their business performance and described the range of services available. The manual also explained how ICL wanted to work in partnership with customers to gain a greater understanding of their business and tailor services that would meet their changing business requirements. As part of the partnership programme, ICL would work closely with the customer's own support staff to improve their skills and enable them to make a greater contribution to business success.

BENEFITS OF THE PROGRAMME

The customer response strategy was a wide-ranging programme that focused on the need to provide the customer with increasingly higher standards of service. The programme provided both ICL and the customer with important business benefits. The benefits to ICL included:

- improved standards of service to all customers
- powerful product and service differentiation
- improved and stronger relationships with customers
- consistent standards of service delivery from all local branches
- improved customer perceptions of product reliability
- cost-effective service delivery
- more effective use of service resources

- better use of the branch network
- improved service delivery times
- added-value service for customers
- potential to increase service revenue and profitability.

Customers benefited too from:

- simpler service administration through a single point of contact
- greater service and product reliability
- higher standards of service
- reduced downtime and more effective use of systems
- better use of their own service support staff
- services tailored to their own business requirements.

KEY MANAGEMENT TASKS

Like the incident management service described in Chapter 13, the programme has two main elements – the infrastructure to deliver the service and the personal skills to provide the right level of customer care.

The infrastructure requires a significant investment to ensure that the service can be delivered rapidly and efficiently throughout the country. Depending on the complexity of the project, it might include:

- communications to provide a rapid response to customer queries and put the service into operation
- a trained support team to deliver the service
- quality-controlled suppliers to support the direct response team
- a control centre to manage the operations and co-ordinate the response
- a network of contacts and suppliers to provide the specialist services that form part of the response.

Skilled staff are essential to the effective delivery of the service. The skills requirements would include:

- incident management skills to deal with customer queries
- project management skills to co-ordinate and implement a response
- technical skills to deliver the service
- communications skills to co-ordinate the elements of the programme.

SUMMARY

Technology provides a valuable support to personal skills in delivering the highest standards of customer service. Technology can allow the centralisation of customer response through a national call reception centre and the introduction of centres of excellence, providing consistent support to customers nationwide. The implementation of a company-wide customer care training programme ensured that all staff were customer focused and balanced the investment in technology. Considerable infrastructure and communications resources are required to deliver a consistent standard of service round the clock, but the investment in this level of service can result in high levels of customer satisfaction.

Self-assessment checklist

- What types of customer queries do you handle?

- What is the personal or business impact of these queries?

- How could technology help you provide support?

- What are the resource and investment implications of a support service?

- Could you deliver the support services yourself or would you need to co-ordinate the activities of third party specialists?

- Do your staff have the skills to deliver the different elements of the service?

15

USING COMMUNICATIONS TO ENHANCE A SERVICE

When First Direct introduced round the clock telephone banking, it was a breakthrough in customer service. Customers enjoy a personal service whenever they choose to do business and they can carry out transactions without visiting a branch. First Direct utilised the power of communications to improve personal service, a move that ran counter to the trends in the rest of the high street banking system.

Technology had been used to automate many traditional banking processes and the result had been a reduction in personal contact and a loss of identity. Automatic tellers, direct debits and other forms of automation meant that customers no longer needed to visit their branch. Although that might have increased efficiency and allowed the banks to improve their productivity and reduce costs, it meant that they had lost contact with their customers.

There is a parallel in the insurance business where companies had traditionally maintained a field force of collectors and agents calling on households. Direct debits and other forms of automated payment enabled the insurance company to reduce their overheads but lose vital contact.

First Direct's use of technology was innovative in the finance sector. Banks and building societies had invested heavily in information technology (IT) as a means of improving productivity. At one level, IT was seen as a way of freeing staff to deal with customers; there was a clear distinction between front- and back-office duties and IT was seen as a way of dealing with the back-office issues. This enabled banks and building societies to open up the traditional counter area to give staff and customers the chance to meet in a more personal environment. Cash dispensers and other automated processes helped customers deal with routine transactions and freed the counter staff to deal with customer queries, loans and other services. This trend is in line with the long-term business strategy of offering customers a wider portfolio of financial services, including insurance, mortgages, investment advice, stocks and shares, and financial advice, with the aim of building customers for life.

Although the intention was right, the practice ran counter. By providing customers with cash dispensers, increased levels of direct debiting and other facilities for automated transactions, customers had less reason for visiting a branch, and contact was reduced rather than increased.

Many customers felt that they were simply account numbers and that personal service was a thing of the past. First Direct focused clearly on what it saw were the customers' real needs – a personal service at a convenient time for the customer, with a high degree of flexibility. The concept was simple – 24-hour banking by telephone. A customer rang up at any time and was able to carry out a wide range of transactions over the telephone. Far from being an impersonal telephone service, the First Direct contact was perceived as a friendly and personal service where the customer was treated as an individual, rather than a number.

HOW THE DIRECT APPROACH CAN BE USED

The 'direct' approach is now being found in a number of other markets and it can be used to meet different scenarios:

- Customers carry out specific transactions which do not depend on specialist skills.
- Computers provide all the customer information necessary to carry out transactions. Customer details are held on personal computer and can be accessed by any member of the telephone team.
- The customer sees convenience as an important aspect of the service and this convenience is not available through other forms of service delivery. In this case, customers would have to visit a branch and they may not have time, or the location could be difficult.
- The service can be positioned as prompt, flexible and personal and can be tailored to the needs of individual customers.
- Quality of personal service is seen as more important than location.
- People and resources can be concentrated in specific areas, rather than scattered around a branch network.
- The service does not have to be located in a particular area and it does not have to be situated near the mechanism for delivering the service; for example, telephone banking does not require a high street location.
- The service can be branded although it has no physical existence for the customer. This runs contrary to the traditional feeling of the banks that oak panel and marble were essential to the image of stability they wished to convey.

PROGRAMME OBJECTIVES

In setting up a service like this, there are a number of important considerations:

- to deliver a quality service to the customer
- to offer the customer maximum convenience
- to provide customers with a prompt, flexible service
- to utilise the power of the computer and the telephone to deliver a personal service
- to compete effectively with traditional methods of service delivery.

IMPLEMENTING THE PROGRAMME

First Direct was a separate division of Midland Bank established to deal with a specific group of customers who were recruited through national advertising and direct marketing. The service was built around network computers and call centre technology. Both were proven technologies, but they had not previously been used in banking. The network computers enabled staff to access customer files as soon as the customer called and to update these files with the latest transaction. Staff had full information on the customer and were able to quickly refer to all the personal and account information they needed. By linking telephones and computer technology, staff were able to deliver higher standards of service. Training was a key element in the development of the service. Staff had to have bank experience as well as customer service skills so that they received a highly personal service.

Direct Line Insurance carved out a profitable niche in the car insurance market by offering customers a highly efficient telesales and claims handling operation. Rather than contact a broker or a traditional insurance company direct the customer was able to benefit from a professional, no-frills operation. By reducing its overheads and not having to support a salesforce or a branch network, the company was able to offer an extremely competitive service. When prospects called, their enquiry was handled by trained sales staff who worked through a planned sequence of questions to ensure the customer received an accurate quote. The quote was handled on computer and was immediate. If the customer accepted the quote, the policy was immediately put into effect and no further action was needed.

Claims were handled in the same straightforward way. The customer phoned in, described the incident and the claim would be dealt with rapidly. This standard of service enabled Direct Line to post good profits and set a standard that other insurance companies tried to follow. Telebanking and direct insurance quotations are beginning to be introduced by competitors, but the standards for customer service have already been established.

BENEFITS OF THE PROGRAMME

Putting the programme into operation provided important benefits for both client and service provider. Customers had a service that was focused on their needs:

- The service provided the highest levels of convenience and flexibility.
- Customers could deal with their financial affairs in the most convenient way.
- They were able to have access to a personal adviser who could deal with any aspect of their financial affairs.
- Financial affairs could be handled at times that were convenient to the customer.
- Customers could make transactions and get an immediate picture of their situation.

The benefits to the bank were equally important:

- They were able to reach a new market who were looking for a specific type of service.
- It enabled the company to take advantage of technology to deliver a highly efficient service.
- The company could concentrate its resources by utilising technology to deliver a consistent nationwide service to every customer.
- The investment in technology and communications set up strong entry barriers that deterred competition.

KEY MANAGEMENT ACTIONS

- Identify how communications can be used to improve a service.
- Assess how customer needs can be met better by effective communications.
- Integrate telecommunications and computing resources to provide the right level of customer response and service.
- Develop an infrastructure to support effective service delivery.
- Develop service criteria that reflect customer needs.
- Train staff in customer care skills as well as product/service specific skills.
- Measure the performance of service delivery.

SUMMARY

First Direct have used information technology and communications in an innovative way, developing a new customer focused service that has improved customer contact, rather than reduced it. The 'direct' approach is now being used by other companies and providing them with successful, profitable business. The service provides high levels of customer convenience and allows a company to deliver consistently high standards of service to all customers, wherever they are located.

Self-assessment checklist

- Can you substitute a direct telephone-based service for any of your customer-facing sales operations?

- What are the key customer requirements for such a service?

- How would the change impact on customers?

- What are the likely perceptions of a telephone-based service?

- Could the telephone-based service be integrated with traditional services?

- What infrastructure would you require to deliver the service?

- What are the main skills requirements?

- Can standards of service be measured?

16

CUSTOMER CLUBS

If you want to make your customers feel welcome, make them members of a club and offer them benefits that reward their loyalty. A club is one of the most effective forms of relationship marketing, helping you to strengthen relationships with your customers and focusing activities on them.

Book clubs like Executive World are among the more obvious forms of customer club – members receive a magazine every two to three months which gives them a useful insight into the books that are available and they pay special discount prices for the books that they select. As well as the regular choice of business books, club members are also offered products from the book clubs in the group, as well as selections from music clubs and other related activities. In this way the club is able improve the profile of its membership and use this database to cross-sell other products.

WHEN THE CLUB APPROACH IS APPROPRIATE

There are a number of scenarios when clubs and other forms of relationship marketing are important:

- when your customers make regular high value purchases and you want to retain their business; the British Airways Executive Club and other frequent travellers clubs are good examples
- when you have customers in a specific age group and you wish to retain their loyalty for life; young savers clubs are examples of this
- when there is an opportunity to add value to basic technological support services; the Spies Hecker Colour Club described in this chapter is an example
- when members pay a single annual fee for a service and you wish to retain their membership – motoring organisations such as the AA and RAC for example
- when there is an opportunity to make regular offers and sell related products to specific groups of consumers with special interests – book clubs or wine clubs for example;

- when there is an opportunity to differentiate a product or service by offering customers added-value services that enhance the basic product or service – user groups for example
- when there is an opportunity to offer regular subscribers special benefits – the *Sunday Times* readers discount card for example.

The format of a customer club is extremely flexible and it is suitable for consumer, business-to-business and service markets. In this chapter, we focus on a business-to-business club – the Spies Hecker Colour Club.

BACKGROUND

Spies Hecker are a European manufacturer of vehicle refinishing systems and part of the worldwide Hoechst Chemicals Group. They run colour clubs for customers in a number of European countries and the UK operation was able to take advantage of the experience of its French and German counterparts to set up a new club from scratch. In the UK, Spies Hecker products are marketed to 'premier' bodyshops or vehicle accident repair centres. These are bodyshops which have invested in equipment such as low-bake ovens that are essential to high quality. Premier bodyshops concentrate on the quality end of the market, offering high standards of repair and refinishing. They can be compared with the 'under-the-arches' body repair and respray centres.

Choice of paint is important to premier bodyshops because they depend on technologically advanced paints to achieve high finishing standards. The market is extremely competitive and there are a number of technically advanced suppliers competing for market share. As well as paint, the manufacturers also need to supply their bodyshops with accurate colour information. Colour information ensures that a refinisher is able to accurately match the colour of the original when he is respraying a car. The concept behind the Colour Club was to offer bodyshops a range of unique colour resources that would enable them to improve their own colour-matching performance. This would enable Spies Hecker to position themselves as business partners and improve customer loyalty by offering direct business benefits.

SETTING OBJECTIVES

The key business objectives were to:

- secure customer loyalty in a competitive market

- build partnership with customers by improving their colour performance
- raise awareness of Spies Hecker as a supplier of products and services for quality refinishing
- increase levels of quality contact with customers
- improve understanding of customer needs.

IMPLEMENTATION

The club was launched by a combination of direct marketing and salesforce activity. Customers were offered membership of the club plus a range of benefits in return for an annual subscription. The benefits included:

- an updated edition of the Spies Hecker Colour Yearbook – an easy-to-use reference guide to refinishing colours. This single guide would replace a cumbersome system of multiple reference books that had to be updated by the bodyshop. The yearbook contained all the latest colours for the year and was updated by a members' support programme that provided latest available information so that the bodyshop could work on new models or new colours as soon as they were available
- exclusive access to a colour hotline which provided members with technical information or advice and guidance whenever they needed it
- training vouchers – members received discounts off colour skills courses
- regular technical bulletins that offered useful advice.

As well as the technical support provided through the club, members were also offered privileged discounts on the company's products together with a range of social activities that increased personal contact and added further value to the club.

This club offered its members a wide range of social and business benefits in return for a membership subscription. Although many clubs are offered free to members, they may not offer such high levels of technical support, so a balance has to be struck between value and cost.

Although the UK Colour Club was a new development for Spies Hecker, they had the model of other European clubs to draw on. The project was introduced over a four-month period and involved the development of a format for the club, the launch of the club to customers and the initial administration of the club to ensure that it operated effectively.

The original format for the club was based on an approach already tried in other territories but was refined through market research. Potential members were given the opportunity to discuss the format of the club in a series of focus groups run by a professional market research specialist. The focus groups were asked to rank the importance of various elements of the club and were asked to indicate the membership fee they would be willing to pay in exchange for a range of benefits.

The research enabled Spies Hecker to fine-tune the club offer and to develop a strategy for launching the club. The success of the club depended on high initial uptake so that it would operate as a viable proposition from the start. It was also important to get members to agree to an annual subscription and renewal date that could be tied to the launch of the next issue of the colour information.

The launch was targeted at existing customers but was also used to attract new prospects and win competitive business through added-value offers. The programme was to be launched through a combination of direct mail and salesforce contact. Direct mail was used as a means of quickly getting information into the hands of all customers. The salesforce followed up with visits to selected customers so that the deal could be secured quickly.

The salesforce was not used on every customer because it was not experienced in dealing with this kind of business service. The salesforce was primarily a technical salesforce used to explaining product benefits to the bodyshop manager, but the marketing of the customer club required a sales presentation at a different level – the salesforce would be selling to senior managers and presenting business benefits. This required different sales skills so it was important that Spies Hecker carried out training that would enable the salesforce to carry out the task. There was also a feeling that time spent selling the club concept was not time spent selling and it therefore required an incentive programme to ensure the right level of commitment.

PROGRAMME BENEFITS

The Colour Club was designed to benefit both customer and company. The benefits to Spies Hecker included:

- improved customer loyalty
- higher levels of customer contact
- stronger business relationships
- better colour skills and therefore increased satisfaction with the product
- improved technical and colour skills in the bodyshop. This in turn improves the reputation of the supplier and makes for stronger branding
- the programme is capable of extension into a preferred supplier situation. Here a manufacturer can work with a group of distributors or customers to improve overall performance and reach agreed standards, for example as an

authorised distributor.

These benefits are important in a business-to-business scenario because they provide the bodyshop with a specific business benefit rather than just a sales incentive. Customers also benefited directly from club membership:

- they were able to improve the colour skills of their refinishing staff and that is a key factor in bodyshop marketing. Customer satisfaction depends on the quality of finish – the right surface and, most important, the right colour. Research had shown that colour matching was the single most important factor, not only because of customer satisfaction, but because it improved productivity and reduced waste. Too long spent mixing or respraying a car because the colour matching was inaccurate hit directly at profitability and therefore the colour club made a direct impact.
- better information – information on new colour developments is vital to a bodyshop. It needs to be able to tackle any job – even a brand new car can be damaged in the first week after launch. The club service that provided immediate access to the latest colour information was a vital addition to the regular flow of information.
- telephone hotline support – research had also shown that technical support was one of the most important features of a customer relationship. When a technician was in the middle of a complex job and hit a problem, he needed advice fast. Telephone hotline access to experts was therefore a valuable benefit. A telephone advisory service had been available but the club version was free and promised immediate response.
- opportunities to meet other specialists – initial research had shown that people in the refinishing business regarded regular contact and exchange of ideas as important. The club offer of regular business meetings in a local venue provided a valuable forum for discussion, while the offer of trips to specific exhibitions or centres such as the Citroen Design Centre or an American bodyshop exhibition provided an opportunity to keep up to date with industry best practice and to gain an appreciation of the international refinishing scene.

There were significant benefits to Spies Hecker and to the customer and the club is therefore an effective form of customer loyalty.

KEY TASKS

Setting up a customer club in a business-to-business environment does not involve a major investment. The main investment is in selling the concept to customers. The programme requires careful administration to ensure that customers receive the highest standards of service, therefore training in programme administration skills will be important. It is essential that adequate resources are committed to the programme – quality customer relationships are essential to the success of the customer club. The key tasks were to:

- identify the business benefits of the club
- assess the cost of the programme
- appoint a programme co-ordinator
- research customer requirements
- refine the contents of the programme
- develop a launch strategy
- introduce the concept of the programme internally to build commitment
- implement the practical requirements of the programme – the technical hotline, the training programmes and the mechanism for distributing product information
- implement any training programmes required to deliver quality service to club members
- introduce the programme to the salesforce;
- develop a launch programme to ensure high levels of awareness among prospective club members
- operate a launch and sales incentive programme to recruit high membership levels
- implement a programme to ensure that members continue to receive high levels of benefit, and to develop a membership programme that will continue to strengthen relationships.

SUMMARY

Customer clubs are an effective form of relationship marketing that enable a company to add value to their customer services and differentiate a service. Clubs can be targeted at specific sectors of the market and offer valuable opportunities to achieve higher levels of customer contact and stronger business relationships. In business markets, clubs should offer customers tangible business benefits and help to achieve high levels of customer retention. Clubs must be active and companies should ensure that customers receive a constant stream of offers to maintain interest.

Self-assessment checklist

- Would a customer club be appropriate for your business?
- What elements would you include in a customer club?
- Could the club be customised for different sectors of the market?
- How would a club add value to customer relationships?
- Do you have the resources to manage a club or should you outsource club management?
- What is the time-scale for your club?
- Would the club offer greater opportunities for customer contact?

17

HELPING CUSTOMERS IMPROVE THEIR BUSINESS PERFORMANCE

The best business benefit a company can offer is to help its customers to improve their own marketing performance. That can be achieved through lower prices which make the customer more competitive, training to improve sales skills, making special delivery arrangements so that the customer can respond more quickly to market opportunities, and joint ventures to attack specific sectors of the market. This chapter describes how a number of component manufacturers have worked closely with their customers to improve marketing performance, building stronger business relationships in the process.

RHP Bearings, for example, worked closely with international distributors to take advantage of new opportunities in developing markets, while automotive parts manufacturer, Perrys, introduced a series of customer focused programmes to help other franchised automotive distributors compete more effectively with independent distributors. By assessing their customers' requirements and looking at the business relationships as well as the sales relationship, these companies were able to improve all-round performance.

WHEN THE STRATEGY IS IMPORTANT

This type of support is important in a number of business scenarios:

- Customers are facing increasing levels of competition in their own marketplace. Your business prospects would be threatened if they were to lose share.
- Customers have significant business opportunities but do not have the resources to take advantage of them. By providing additional skills, resources and services, you enable your customers to compete more effec-

tively.

- Your customers face strong price competition and you do not want to reduce your own prices. By offering a choice of structured discounts and incentives the customer can take advantage of your offer to improve their own pricing.
- Your customers are aiming to improve the speed of their own operations. If your customers are in a market where speed is important – in the repair or service business for example – overnight delivery, high stock levels and preferential stockholding facilities can help them to improve their own delivery service.
- Your customers are successful in sales terms, but they are not running their business profitably. By offering management support or other forms of business support, you can help them improve their productivity and profitability.
- Your customers want to get more of their staff involved in sales and customer service. However, many of them are involved in the basic, but time-consuming process of ordering and chasing delivery. By simplifying administration or introducing computerised ordering and information systems, you can reduce their burden and allow them to concentrate on more productive activities.
- Your customers need to develop new skills to improve their own competitive advantage or tackle new market opportunities. By providing them with training support and skills transfer, you can ensure that they exploit new business opportunities.
- Your own business with customers is threatened by new forms of price competition and you want to strengthen account control by adding value to the business relationship. A range of services that improve customers' business performance can help to move the argument away from price competition to other forms of service.

PROGRAMME OBJECTIVES

In establishing a business support programme, you should set the following objectives:

- Maintain account control by strengthening business relationships.
- Support your customers' marketing and customer service initiatives as a means of increasing your own sales and profitability.
- Ensure that your customers have the skills and support to tackle competitors and achieve their business objectives.

PROGRAMME IMPLEMENTATION

Perrys, a Ford main dealer, had a parts operation which was the largest Ford parts distributor in the UK after Ford itself. The company provided a parts wholesale service to other Ford dealers around the country ensuring that they had a fast, cost-effective parts delivery service to enable them to compete with local independent retailers in their local market. Perrys had a large central parts warehouse and were able to offer regular scheduled deliveries to different parts of the country. In many cases, this was a same day delivery service, or several times a day, depending on local requirements. If the customers needed emergency parts to cope with an urgent breakdown, they could make alternative delivery arrangements so that the local dealer was able to respond quickly.

They also identified another opportunity to improve local service by offering overnight delivery to selected areas. Parts could be ordered before close of business giving Perrys the chance to co-ordinate the orders and plan the optimum delivery route. The parts would be delivered before opening of business. This provided a number of important benefits for the local customer:

- They were able to load their own delivery first thing in the morning and provide their local customers with an early morning delivery service.
- They had all the parts available for their workshop schedules first thing in the morning. This meant that the repairs and service work could be carried out without delay so that the workshop could schedule its own work more efficiently and improve customer satisfaction by handling local customer vehicles on time.
- The local customers were able to offer their customers an enhanced service.

As a second stage in improving customer service, Perrys changed their order processing system. They appointed regular specialists who kept in regular contact with their own customers, keeping them up to date with new developments and understanding more about their business. To simplify the order-taking process, Perrys introduced new telesales techniques. Customers had a choice of direct lines, access via the switchboard, contact with regional specialists via mobile phones or dedicated fax order systems.

The company also set up an on-line ordering system for key customers. The programme was originally piloted through the Perrys group to simplify internal administration. Using public networks the company was able to establish direct links with each of the main branches. The parts contact in each branch could make enquiries about stock available on his or her own terminal, place an order, enquire about prices and initiate a series of actions at the Perrys Parts Centre. The system would allocate the parts to the customer, create collection and delivery documentation, adjust stock levels and generate delivery notes and invoices for the customer. The customer got an immediate response and was able to simplify the entire parts order process. By making it easier to order, Perrys simplified the customer's own business performance.

Suppliers of construction equipment like the CASE group are improving customer service by focusing on aftercare service. They aim to provide their customers with the highest standards of service throughout the country. They have a number of choices:

- to set up their own service network, involving a major investment in service infrastructure and skills
- to use the service of an independent service organisation on a third party basis
- to work in partnership with an independent service organisation to establish a joint service network conforming to the supplier's quality standards.

The first option is feasible when the supplier already has an established service operation and simply has to expand it, but this is an option that can be difficult and the operation would have to be scaled up and down to meet different levels of business. The second option – working with an independent – appears to be satisfactory in some circumstances, but the network may be unsuitable and the service provider may not be able to operate to the levels of quality that the supplier needs. The third option, working in partnership with a network of independent service organisations, provides a flexible solution and can benefit both parties.

CASE decided to extend the reach of their own service network by setting up a partnership agreement with independent service specialists. The manufacturer supports the service specialists by:

- providing full product training for service staff
- providing full technical support to the service staff
- providing access to the company's service database
- developing service tools to enable the distributor service staff to handle more complex service tasks
- setting up simplified ordering procedures so that service staff quickly get the parts they need
- developing quality standards in conjunction with distributor staff so that the service is delivered to an agreed standard
- setting up a central service reception facility so that customers can easily contact the appropriate service centre to get service anywhere in the country
- communicating the nationwide service network to their customers.

These actions enable the specialists to improve the performance of their own service operations and to provide the level of service needed by the manufacturer. The specialists, for their part, agreed to:

- participate in the manufacturer's training programme
- conform to quality standards that were jointly agreed
- maintain adequate stock levels to provide adequate service cover
- give priority to the company's service business
- comply with response levels.

The partnership agreement benefits both parties:

- The manufacturer acquires a quality nationwide service network with the minimum investment and is able to provide a high level of service to customers.
- The dealers improve their own service performance and gain access to additional sources of service business.

Traigon, a company specialising in security packaging for the financial sector and the security market, sell their products in Europe through independent distributors. Their distributors have considerable experience in selling related products to financial institutions, but they do not have a depth of knowledge of the Traigon product. When they identified an opportunity to build business with the domestic banks, they approached Traigon to help them develop a joint presentation when they were negotiating with corporate purchasing teams at head office level. Traigon were able to provide the technical and marketing expertise plus marketing communications support to win the business.

RHP Bearings, part of an international engineering group, worked with a selected group of engineering distributors in the UK to help them win a major parts and service contract with a major public organisation. The distributor had a network of branches strategically located near each of the customer's main depots; they had the product range to meet the customer's demands and their staff were already dealing with the customer on *ad hoc* purchases. To make an effective pitch for the business, the distributors needed to strengthen their business in a number of areas:

- scheduled, guaranteed delivery without major stockholding
- technical support and backup
- availability of special products
- competitive prices on high volume purchases
- emergency service to keep the customer operations running.

RHP was able to provide the continuity of supply and the backup the distributor needed by analysing the customer's scheduled and emergency stock requirements and developing supply schedules which would enable the distributor to provide guaranteed cover in a cost-effective way. The partnership arrangement benefited both parties because RHP was able to increase its business with the distributor without the cost of setting up a supply network to service a large multi-site customer and the distributors were able to build on their existing local relationship with the customer to increase their business and secure a major contract.

BENEFITS OF THE PROGRAMME

Programmes like this have a mutual benefit – they enable a manufacturer to improve overall sales and marketing penetration by improving customers' marketing performance. The customer – usually a partner or a distributor – is able to run his or her business more efficiently and more profitably and builds closer relations with the manufacturer. The manufacturer may also gain access to new markets or be able to offer service or coverage that would not be possible using his or her own resources.

KEY MANAGEMENT ACTIONS

- Identify gaps in your own service or market penetration that can be filled by working with third parties.
- Identify suitable customers who could provide access to those opportunities.
- Assess their strengths and weaknesses as potential partners.
- Assess the support requirements needed to improve their business performance or help them meet standards.
- Put a support programme into operation.
- Incorporate a formal support agreement if necessary.

SUMMARY

Manufacturers and distributors are improving their own market penetration by working closely with customers to help them improve their own business performance. Support can take a number of different forms, including business support, training, marketing support, joint ventures or improved delivery service and pricing. By focusing on the customer's business requirements, the manufacturer can develop a tailored service that builds effective working relationships and increases account control.

Self-assessment checklist

- Can you identify opportunities to improve your customers' business performance?

- Would a support programme increase your own market penetration?

- Would customer support improve account control?

- What form of support would be most effective?

- Do you have the resources to deliver this support?

- Can you identify opportunities for joint ventures?

- Would simple strategies such as lowering prices, increasing discounts or improving delivery performance help to make your customers more competitive?

18

HELPING YOUR CUSTOMERS MAKE BUSINESS DECISIONS

Improving your customer's skills in areas of complexity and uncertainty demonstrates high levels of professionalism and customer care. By working with customers to improve their skills at a strategic level, you not only help to improve working relationships, you gain a valuable insight into their business objectives.

The IBM Executive Briefing Centre was set up to help clients develop a more informed approach to decision making. IBM identified that clients who were fully informed about information systems would make effective decisions that would reflect their own business requirements as well as practical information systems considerations. Although this type of exercise helps to position IBM and the suppliers who provide this type of service as professional consultants, it will also demonstrate that the company understands the customers' business concerns.

Telecommunications specialists run briefing sessions for telecommunications managers and senior executives at venues around the country. The intention was the same – to ensure that customers make the right decisions about telecommunications systems.

The engineering business contains many examples of companies who help their clients to make informed decisions about new materials or new processes. Although briefing centres are predominately found in high-technology businesses, they can be equally applied to the service sector and to any activity where the purchase decision is complex.

WHEN BRIEFING STRATEGIES ARE APPROPRIATE

A number of scenarios can be used to identify opportunities for introducing customer briefings:

- Customers have to make fundamental decisions about the future direction of their business. The new product or service will have a significant impact on the future direction of their business, and it is important that customers understand the full implications. Purchasing is not simply a matter of replacing an existing product or service, or changing suppliers, it will reshape the business. Customers will have to reconsider how their future product range will shape up, what markets they can enter and how they will manage their business in the new environment.

- The product or service will have an impact on the organisational structure or working practices. New manufacturing techniques, new materials or new technology could require a fundamental change in working practice. The customer will not be making a strategic change in direction, but will be doing the same things in a different way. It is essential that the management team understand how they will have to change their organisation to take advantage of the new developments. Failure to change means that they may only partially benefit. The change could involve retraining or new investment or reorganisation.

- The product or service is based on a new technology and the customer has no experience of assessing its cost-effectiveness. New technology could offer major benefits but cost more initially. The management team may dismiss the product or service as too expensive but not realise the full cost implications. A briefing session could help them to understand the full through-life implications which may benefit the company. Briefing sessions would help them to assess the product from a different point of view.

- The product or service is part of a complete solution that provides broad-ranging business benefits for the customer. It is vital for the supplier to explain how all the elements of the package work together.

- New legislation will have an impact on the customer and the supplier provides a product or service that will help customers meet requirements. The company's expertise can help the customer to understand the implications of the legislation and develop a strategy for dealing with it.

- The supplier has skills that the customer wishes to acquire. Skills and knowledge transfer are an important part of executive briefing.

- A supplier wishes to demonstrate professionalism. Executive briefing centres can help to position a company as an expert in a specific product or service area, building closer relationships with clients.

- Consultancy is an important part of the total product and service package; briefing sessions are an integral part of the consultancy process.

- A company wants to build partnership with key customers and uses the briefing sessions to build a better understanding of the customer's business processes.

SETTING OBJECTIVES

An executive briefing session meets a number of key business objectives. These include:

- ensuring that a customer has adequate information to make business decisions
- positioning a company as an expert in the field
- improving long-term business relationships with customers
- demonstrating an understanding of customers' business processes
- building effective relationships at senior executive level with key decision makers
- providing opportunities to improve customer satisfaction through skills and knowledge transfer
- improving long-term customer satisfaction by providing customers with an effective business solution
- providing opportunities for quality contacts with customers
- providing opportunities to positively influence the decision-making process.

THE BRIEFING PROCESS

Communicating partnership through seminars

At a seminar, a number of speakers make presentations to the audience and may participate in question and answer sessions. The audience can be invited to a 'closed' event, or may choose to attend an 'open' event. The seminar can be a self-contained event or it may form part of a wider event such as an exhibition or conference. You may be one of a number of companies presenting at the seminar – the other presenters may include your competitors – or you may limit the presenters to people from your own organisation. The more control you have over the event and the presenters, the more you can influence the response and attitudes of the audience. However, it may be more appropriate to present your message within the context of an independent, authoritative seminar where your presentation will be seen as impartial.

In deciding what form the seminar should take, you should consider the following questions:

- Will the audience include the types of company and the target audience you want to reach? If you are inviting delegates, you decide the audience, but if the seminar is open, you need to know who the organisers are targeting.

- Does the seminar have a theme and programme that corresponds with the values of your customer focus programme? For example, an open seminar on 'Manufacturing in the '90s' would be appropriate for an engineering company which wished to reach key manufacturing decision makers.
- Does the seminar have the right degree of authority? If the manufacturing seminar was organised by an official body such as the Department of Trade and Industry, that would add a degree of authority to the presenting companies.
- Do the other seminar presentations complement your message and reinforce your theme?
- Will the seminar format provide you with enough time to present your arguments in detail? If not, how easily can you follow up the seminar audience?

There are a number of important actions to ensure that the seminar meets your communications objectives:

- Set specific objectives for the seminar, for example, to raise awareness of the importance of your proposal.
- Select speakers with the authority and status to present strategic messages.
- Ensure that the presentation focuses on concerns and business issues that are important to your customers.
- Incorporate the positioning messages that stress the strategic benefits of working with your company.

Using the example of the fictitious 'Manufacturing in the '90s' seminar, this is an example of how an engineering company might utilise the seminar to reach key contacts in industry.

'Manufacturing in the '90s' is run by an independent conference organiser in conjunction with a government body such as the Department of Trade and Industry. The organisers have assembled a group of presenters from industry, government and the academic world and have invited an audience of senior executives from Britain's leading manufacturing companies. The speakers cover strategically important topics such as new developments in manufacturing technology, the importance of information systems, changing investment criteria and human resource implications of the likely changes. Within the context of the seminar, a presentation on the strategic benefits of partnership is appropriate and helps to provide senior executives with a broad perspective. The seminar positions partnership as an integral element of competitive manufacturing management. The company's paper is presented by the managing director and provides a unique opportunity for high-level contact with other senior executives.

After the seminar, the company takes the opportunity to maintain communication by mailing management summaries of the seminar papers to delegates and important customers or prospects who were unable to attend. Telephone research conducted before and after the seminar revealed that awareness of the benefits of partnership had increased by 18 per cent, and this provided a valuable basis for planning the next stage of the communications programme.

Executive briefings

Executive briefings are similar in many ways to seminars, but they are completely under your control. For example, the briefings can adopt the same format as a seminar, with a number of different speakers from your company presenting on related topics. However, the content of the presentations is completely under your control and can be tailored to the business needs of individual customers. A number of larger organisations have set up special executive briefing centres to concentrate on this important aspect of business development. The briefing centres are often located in converted country houses with full presentation facilities, accommodation, catering and areas for discussion and relaxation. The intention is to create an environment where busy executives can get away from day-to-day pressures and concentrate on issues of strategic importance.

An environment like that is helpful, but not essential. Management briefings can be held on your customers' premises, at your offices or in a conference-type location such as a hotel or business centre. It is however important to provide an area where the meeting can take place without disturbance in an atmosphere that is conducive to strategic thinking.

The briefing is designed to bring executives up to date with issues that are seen as important to their business and to help them decide how to assess the potential of an issue such as partnership within their organisation. The agenda for an executive briefing on partnership might include the following sessions:

- the business benefits of partnership
- how is partnership currently used within the industry?
- is partnership relevant to your organisation?
- the management implications of partnership
- assessing the potential for partnership
- a timetable and action programme for implementing partnership.

As well as demonstrating your understanding of your customer's business and your willingness to help them improve their business performance, a briefing session can encourage open discussion on your customers' business needs and improve working relationships. The executive briefing gives your customers the opportunity to decide whether they can work comfortably with you and demonstrates that partnership depends on close working relationships and an atmosphere of trust. To help customers get the optimum benefit from executive briefings, provide them with workbooks, case histories and models to use in planning their own programmes.

Management reports

Management reports can be issued to different members of the target audience to explain complex issues and outline the main topics customers should review. Many management reports are based on market research and provide customers with an overview of current practice. A management report is not a promotional publication; it should be written in a neutral tone and it should offer customers objective advice that will help them to make effective decisions and, by improving the quality of the decision-making process, you can ensure that your proposals are evaluated professionally. Management reports demonstrate that you understand your own and your partner's business and that you are prepared to help your customers improve the quality of their own decision making.

An information systems company produced a management report on the management implications of Just-In-Time (JIT) manufacturing processes to ensure that their customers were aware of their own responsibilities. Research had shown that companies who adopted JIT, without considering the full potential impact on their business, tended to blame their information system for problems that were actually due to lack of understanding and poor management. The management report was structured as a briefing document for different members of the management team. It explained that the JIT approach to manufacturing required the commitment and involvement of the whole management team. JIT decisions were shown to be wide ranging, involving the chief executive and board director, together with managers and executives responsible for production, finance, purchasing and marketing. The report explained the potential benefits of JIT, illustrating them with statistics and conclusions from the information system manufacturer's experience in implementing JIT in its own factories. The report then outlined an agenda for discussing JIT and highlighted the critical management decisions. The report was widely used in manufacturing industry and was adopted as a standard by a number of professional institutes who were trying to improve management standards.

Management reports play an important role in building effective relations with contacts at all levels in the customer organisation by promoting informed, thorough discussion of the potential of issues facing the customer:

- They demonstrate to senior executives that your proposals have taken their business issues into consideration.
- They help middle managers to make informed decisions about key business issues and reduce the risk of poor decision-making that is narrowly focused.

- They can help purchasing executives to take a broader view of the importance of a proposal by demonstrating the wide-ranging implications and business benefits that can result.

SUMMARY

This chapter has explained how you can use high-level management briefings to improve relationships with your customers and position your company as a strategic supplier. Seminars and management briefings are valuable techniques for communicating with senior executives and this form of direct contact can be supplemented by published management guides. The programme helps your customers to improve skills at a level that would not normally be available through conventional training.

Self-assessment checklist

- What complex issues do your customers face where you can improve their understanding?

- Can you identify open seminars that would be appropriate for your target audience and your message?

- Can you run your own seminars, and what form would they take?

- Are you able to bring together important executives from potential customers?

- What is their current understanding of your proposals and your organisation?

- How will an executive briefing improve their understanding?

- Do you have the resources to produce management reports on important issues?

- What role will the management report play in the development of improved relationships?

- What are the key issues to be covered in the report?

19

MAKING IT EASIER FOR CUSTOMERS TO BUY

This chapter looks at ways in which you can help your customers do business by making it easier for them to buy from you. Many companies put up artificial barriers to trade by making their ordering procedures complex, failing to provide adequate product information or setting up complex procedures for billing. This chapter describes a number of techniques that will help your customers to select, order and obtain products easily.

SIMPLIFYING ORDERING PROCEDURES

Ordering costs both supplier and purchaser money, so anything that can simplify the ordering process will save your customers money and improve customer relationships. When ICI were assessing the benefits of electronic payments systems, they estimated that they were raising vast amounts of paperwork with thousands of suppliers. This exercise would have kept a large purchasing department fully occupied and prevented the purchasing staff from carrying out anything more than basic operations. But, by utilising an electronics payment system, they were able to reduce the paperwork mountain and ensure that their purchasing staff were able to concentrate on improving supplier performance.

Recent developments in business process re-engineering show that it is possible to improve this process still further. Ford Trucks worked in partnership with key components suppliers to develop a system that put the onus on the suppliers to decide when they should deliver components. The suppliers were able to access Ford's manufacturing schedules to plan their own production schedules. The logical outcome of the process is here where the supplier acts as an internal department supplying to requirements, rather than responding to *ad hoc* requests. The purchaser does not have to raise paperwork or even plan schedules – that is taken care of by the supplier. Although this may be too advanced for most supplier/customer relationships, the principles of applying information can be applied to most purchasing scenarios.

ON-LINE ORDERING

With the growth in computerised manufacturing and stock control systems, companies are using on-line ordering to simplify administration. A motor dealership with a number of regional branches used on-line ordering to speed up and simplify their parts ordering procedures. Branch staff were able to access the central parts department computer over public communications networks; they could get immediate information on the stock available of various parts and place their orders. Stock levels were automatically adjusted and the system produced delivery notes, invoices and picking instructions. This process cut out several layers of paperwork and speeded up ordering and delivery.

The on-line ordering process can be extended to key customers with its logical conclusion in the Ford system described earlier. On-line systems depend on effective communication links between supplier and buyer; although detailed guidelines are outside the scope of this book, companies can either set up their own dedicated networks or utilise public networks.

Just-In-Time (JIT) is a process of meeting customer delivery and stockholding requirements by integrating planning, communications and distribution. Customers can reduce their own stockholding levels and maintain adequate cover for their product requirements because suppliers plan their own production levels and distribution levels in line with customer requirements. When customers need stock, it is delivered, literally, just-in-time.

JIT depends on close co-operation between supplier and customer and utilises computerised production control systems to exchange information that is used for planning. JIT plays an important role in key account management by providing the customer with security of supply.

NATIONAL ENQUIRY CENTRES

Simplifying customer access can improve customer convenience. By creating a central contact point for all customer enquiries, you can ensure that every incoming customer contact is handled efficiently. This is particularly appropriate for companies who have a number of separate locations or who are organised by product group. At the national enquiry centre all incoming calls are handled by a central reception centre and routed to the appropriate specialist. The customer does not have to waste time trying to track down the right contact. The centre should handle incoming calls for queries such as:

- product information
- technical information

- service requests
- literature
- complaints
- estimates and ordering
- delivery
- accounts.

Many of these calls would be routed direct to the appropriate department, but an increasing number of companies are making the receptionist responsible for customer contact and incident management. For example, if a key customer makes a service request, the receptionist takes the basic details and arranges for a specialist to call the customer back within an agreed time-scale. The receptionist may go further and maintain contact with the customer until the service problem has been resolved. The process is known as incident management and helps to reassure the customer that appropriate action is being taken.

Quality processes can be applied to call reception. For example, companies would be assessed on:

- time to answer the call
- time to respond to the customer
- time to achieve a satisfactory result.

The national enquiry centre is a valuable method of ensuring that the customer receives a consistent standard of quality service on every contact.

FREEPHONE/LOCAL CALL RATES

The process of simplifying access can be handled on a much smaller scale by:

- offering your key customers freephone access to specialist services such as technical queries, service requests, or ordering
- offering your customers a single access number at local call rates. This service can be arranged with your telecommunications supplier.

These facilities allow smaller companies to offer their customers simple access without major investment.

PRODUCT INFORMATION

Clear up-to-date product information is vital to effective customer relationships. The marketing communications specialists on your team should take responsibility for managing the quality of all product information, including:

- technical literature
- catalogues
- technical updates
- product proposals.

CUSTOMISED PRODUCTS

The process can be taken even further by developing a range of products that are customised to individual accounts or branded in the customer' own design. 'Own label' products not only simplify the customer's ordering procedures, they demonstrate that you can work in close co-operation and provide you with greater account control. Customisation can take a number of forms:

- modifying the product
- repackaging the product to suit the customer's own logistics systems
- producing 'own label' versions of the product to simplify and enhance the customer's marketing performance.

REGIONAL AND LOCAL STOCKISTS

If your customers have branches around the country, it may help them to have local stocks to cover service and maintenance requirements. For example, a construction equipment manufacturer supplying its products to contractors needs to have an effective local network of parts and service depots so that they can reduce customer downtime. By offering customers like this access to your own local distribution network, you can ensure that their customers receive a high standard of local service.

CUSTOMISED ADMINISTRATION

If your customer is buying a large number of separate items from you, you can simplify their administrative burden in a number of ways:

- providing 'single line' invoices for groups of different purchases
- integrating your accounts system with theirs so that they receive financial information in a compatible format

- using electronic data interchange to reduce paperwork.

SUMMARY

Making it easier for your customers to buy is a sure way of improving customer satisfaction. Electronic ordering and payments systems, for example, can reduce mountains of paperwork. Communications also make it easier for your key customers to obtain up-to-date commercial and delivery information and lay the foundation for processes such as Just-In-Time which enable you to build even stronger customer links. You can also go further and develop customised products that are unique to the customer. Providing your customers with a single point of access for all enquiries makes it easier for them to do business and allows you to control the quality of customer contact. Customers with branches around the country or a requirement for delivering a local service to their own customers can take advantage of your local networks.

Self-assessment checklist

- Can you use technology or communications to simplify your customers' administrative procedures?

- Do you have the technology to provide customers with on-line access to production and delivery information?

- Have you considered using Just-In-Time techniques to strengthen relationships with key accounts?

- Can you provide your customers with a central point of contact for all enquiries?

- How could you apply quality processes to customer reception?

- Have you evaluated your product information for ease of use?

- Would your customers benefit from a range of customised products?

- Can your customers make use of your distribution network to improve their local service?

20

REWARDING LOYAL CUSTOMERS

One of the key objectives of customer focus is to retain customers over the long term. Customers who are satisfied with the level and quality of service they receive are likely to continue buying from the same company. This degree of loyalty can be reinforced by customer retention programmes which reward customers for their loyalty in a way that further enhances customer service. Retention programmes can take many different forms from simple concepts like discounts on repeat purchases, incentives for multiple purchases to more complex frequent user programmes which provide multilevel rewards for customers who continue to use a service.

This chapter looks at different types of incentive schemes available and shows how a frequent user programme can be put into operation. Retention programmes are not just a form of sales incentive, they demonstrate that your organisation cares about its customers and is prepared to reward loyalty.

WHEN LOYALTY PROGRAMMES ARE IMPORTANT

Retention (or loyalty) programmes are important in the following scenarios:

- Customers use the service frequently and the market is competitive.
- The loyalty programme proves to be an important differentiator.
- The retention programme provides an incentive to high levels of repeat purchase. Customers may use the product or service more frequently to gain additional points or prizes in the incentive programme.
- The incentive or reward itself provides an opportunity to demonstrate high levels of customer service. A frequent hotel user programme, for example, gives the customer an assured reservation, fast reception and a range of information to help make the traveller's life easier. Frequent flyer clubs not only give customers points towards free travel, they also include free use of

an executive lounge, simplified booking and check-in procedures. This in itself can increase customer satisfaction.

- The company is competing with other suppliers who offer similar services but do not have a customer service policy.
- The reward programme forms an integral part of the product or service offering.

PROGRAMME OBJECTIVES

A customer retention programme would have the following business objectives:

- to reflect the high standard of customer service available
- to offer customers a valuable reward or incentive for the continued relationship
- to improve customer convenience as well as providing a reward
- to motivate customers to remain loyal to the company
- to provide high levels of customer information as a basis for database marketing programmes and future product development.

A frequent flyer programme run by major airlines is a good example of a long-term customer loyalty programme that meets these objectives. The programmes are focused primarily on business travellers who travel regularly throughout the year. Although they are not spending their own money on travel, they are likely to select an airline that offers them the right level of service and convenience with an additional bonus if the airline includes a personal reward for loyalty.

USING INCENTIVE PROGRAMMES

Incentives and rewards can be used at two levels in a customer focus programme:

- tactically to improve response to communications or build business
- strategically to support long-term branding and build customer loyalty.

It is important to utilise both aspects because incentives and awards are often regarded as simply tactical.

Tactical consumer promotion

Sales promotion can be integrated with advertising and direct marketing campaigns to raise response rates for both initial enquiries and conversions. For example, including a group of special offers which encourage initial enquiry, signing an agreement and paying the first premium. The sales promotion offers help to move the consumer to action and are an integral part of a response programme.

Strategic sales promotion

Strategic incentives can be integrated with relationship marketing programmes to support branding opportunities and build customer loyalty. In the insurance market, for example, special offers can be developed to encourage existing policy-holders to trade up to higher value policies or to try other products in the group. A strategic campaign can operate in a number of ways:

- offering customers and prospects special services or other offers that support core brand qualities
- rewarding existing customers for renewal and repeat business
- using strategic promotions to reactivate lapsed accounts
- offering customers high quality incentives to support the marketing of higher value products
- structuring programmes to suit different customer spending levels.

Strategic incentive programmes can play a valuable role in supporting other customer focus activities.

Sales incentive programmes can be used to focus the salesforce and financial advisers on important customer-facing activities. Sales incentives should be directly related to the current campaigns and can be both tactical and strategic. Tactical incentives could include:

- product sales incentives based on new business generation and policy sales, with a structured scheme related to the number of conversions. This would ensure that the salesforce made the best use of the leads generated through direct marketing and advertising and concentrated on building higher levels of new sales
- structured incentives for target market sales. If the company wants to increase penetration in specific sectors, tie the incentive programme to sales in niche markets and integrate direct marketing and telemarketing activity to increase the chances of success
- short-term incentives to achieve revenue targets
- incentives linked to generation of database information, even though the prospect may not purchase immediately.

Short-term incentives help to focus the salesforce on immediate goals so that they can maintain high levels of sales.

Strategic incentives can help to reduce the salesforce effort over the long term. Customer relationships and high levels of repeat business are critical to the future development of the company and this will require a changing emphasis in the salesforce. The salesforce will be responsible for identifying customer needs and working as consultants rather than selling specific products. The emphasis is on looking at the customer's overall financial requirements so frequent meetings and regular communications are an important part of the process. The calls may not result in immediate sales and this would affect salesforce earning potential.

The incentive scheme should reflect this changing role and could include the following elements:

- structured incentives linked to overall customer performance rather than short-term sales
- incentives linked to training achievement – the training would reflect the new skills of consultancy and relationship marketing which now become more important
- structured incentives linked to high levels of customer retention and repeat business – this helps to change the emphasis from new business at all costs to protection of the business. It represents a change in role from hunter to farmer and it is important to reward the salesforce for their contribution to the success of the programme.

A strategic incentive programme would be integrated with a relationship marketing programme, customer promotional activities that reflect customer retention and a change in the corporate communications programme that reflected the changing relationship between a company and its customers.

FREQUENT BUYER PROGRAMMES

Frequent buyer programmes that also accumulate information on customers are a powerful combination that strengthen the impact of customer focus programmes. An example is the frequent flyer programmes run by most of the major airlines. These provide regular travellers with points for every mile they fly which can be exchanged for free leisure travel. The British Airways programme has added an Executive Club which offers structured rewards to different groups of customers, according to their overall use of airline services. The scheme includes access to preferential seating, arrangements with hotels and car hire companies and access to executive airport lounges.

Retailer Argos operate a programme called Premier Points which issues points to customers for every ten pence they spend. The points are accumulated via a smart card and the customer can use the points to pay for other purchases. Smart card technology is also increasingly used by petrol retailers as a tie in to their collector schemes. Instead of collecting vouchers or tokens, points are accumulated via the card. Multiple food retailers are also beginning to use a similar scheme to reward high spending customers.

ENHANCING FREQUENT BUYER PROGRAMMES

Frequent buyer programmes can be used to build a more complete picture of customers as a basis for detailed customer focus. A smart card can provide detailed knowledge of purchasing patterns that provides a basis for cross-selling other products and services or tailoring products and services to the customer.

SUMMARY

Customer loyalty programmes provide a basis for demonstrating high levels of customer care and differentiating the level of service. It is important that the reward reflects the company's customer service values and increases customer satisfaction. Although incentive programmes are used as part of a sales promotion programme, they also have a strategic role in building effective customer relationships. The most effective customer loyalty programmes not only reward regular customers, they provide information on their purchasing patterns as a basis for future product and service development.

Self-assessment checklist

- How could customer loyalty programmes be used within your customer focus programme?

- How important is repeat purchase to the success of your business?

- Are long-term relationships important to your business?

- Do you have a method of recording your customers' purchasing patterns?

- Could you use technology to improve this kind of data capture?

- What type of reward would be appropriate to your customers?
- Can you link purchase information with other customer information to improve customer focus?

21

TOWARDS PARTNERSHIP

Previous chapters in this book have shown how customer focus strengthens relationships with customers and helps to maintain account control in a competitive market-place. The logical conclusion to this process is partnership – a way of doing business in which supplier and customer trade with each other to achieve mutual business objectives. Partnership replaces the traditional buyer/supplier relationship with a degree of co-operation and trust, and utilises each partner's skills to improve overall competitiveness. Partnership has been given a number of names, including strategic customer alliance, strategic supplier alliance and partnership sourcing.

PARTNERSHIP IN ACTION

Building relationships

An energy supplier and a high-volume electricity user co-operate on process developments that enable the customer to reduce overall manufacturing costs and provide the energy supplier with a long-term supply contract that is not dependent on price negotiations.

Co-operating to win business

A graphic design consultancy and an architectural practice co-operate to win a major retail refurbishing contract. Both partners utilise each other's specialist skills to develop a package of services that provides the ultimate customer with the most effective solution.

Adding value

A car transportation company develops a three-way partnership with car manufacturers and car dealers. As well as providing the basic function of vehicle delivery from plant to dealership, the transport company provides services such as management information to improve communications between manufacturer and dealer, and professional vehicle preparation which help both manufacturer and dealer improve customer satisfaction. The transport company develops a long-term relationship with the manufacturer, and both manufacturer and dealer improve their competitiveness.

Improving local marketing performance

A vehicle paint supplier develops a partnership programme to provide local distributors with skills and systems to improve their business management, marketing and customer service performance. By installing computers and business management systems in its branches, the manufacturer helps to build brand loyalty and improve the quality of service given to the ultimate customer – the bodyshop. The distributor has an opportunity to improve the performance of his own local business.

Developing a joint market

A petrochemical manufacturer co-operates with manufacturing customers to develop the market for a new plastic piping system. By providing high levels of technical and manufacturing support, the petrochemical company ensures that manufacturers understand how to make the best use of the new material. By developing joint product marketing initiatives, the partners are able to educate large-scale users in local government and the utilities of the cost and operational benefits of the new product. As a result, the petrochemical manufacturer increases the market for its new material and builds stronger relationships with customers, while the manufacturers expand the market for their products.

Spreading the risk

A computer company and a management consultancy work in partnership to win a major health authority computer contract. Both parties realise that a successful computerisation programme depends, not just on the best computer solution, but on careful assessment of long-term objectives and the establishment of the right management structure to utilise and manage the computer system. Without a supporting infrastructure, the computer system might have become a 'white elephant'. Close co-operation between both partners ensures that the ultimate customer – the health authority – obtains the right solution and that the partners develop a reputation that enhances their professional credibility.

Reducing costs

An industrial component manufacturer and an engineering company co-operate on a joint development programme to reduce 'through-life' costs of a number of key components. The component manufacturer contributes technical expertise and a close understanding of the engineering company's own customers, while the engineering company provides the component supplier with advice on improving the quality and cost effectiveness of its manufacturing processes. The component supplier ensures long-term customer loyalty, while the energy company reduces its overall costs.

Building links through technology

A travel company introduces a computerised enquiry and reservation system for independent travel agents. The system replaces slow manual systems of obtaining information and booking tickets, and enables independent travel agents to compete effectively with larger multiple travel groups who have access to a corporate reservation system. The travel agents are in a stronger position to win business, while the travel company builds the loyalty of the independent travel agent and improves the quality of service to the consumer.

Differentiating a service

A car insurance company wishes to improve its service to policy holders by offering quality services on body repairs and windscreen replacement. The insurance company works in partnership with leading companies in each sector, helping them to set up business processes and customer reception facilities that will ensure the highest standards of customer service. The specialist suppliers get access to larger markets and higher levels of business, while the insurance company is able to improve its cost position by offering policyholders added value and differentiate its services from price competitors.

This brief outline of partnership cases shows that partnership is relevant to many different types of business – small and large manufacturers, subcontractors, consultancies, distributors and retail outlets. In none of these cases were there formal contractual arrangements, although suppliers had to satisfy strict performance standards. Partnership evolved or occurred because both partners recognised the business benefits that would result.

WHY PARTNERSHIP IS IMPORTANT

Partnership does not happen in isolation; nor do buyers and sellers suddenly decide to change the nature of their relationship. Partnership occurs because there are initiatives from either supplier or buyer driven by a need to improve a company's competitive performance. These driving forces include:

- increasing competition in the market-place
- higher customer expectations
- pressure on costs
- rapid technological change
- competing in wider markets
- need for rapid new product development
- skills shortages
- introduction of new business processes
- focus on core skills.

Increasing competition

Companies are facing increasing competition from many different sources.

- Low cost competitors, particularly from developing economies. Quality is acceptable, in many cases good, but the competitors are operating from a low cost base or taking advantage of new technology or government support to reduce their start-up costs. Examples include the bearing and fastener industries where the Japanese and East Europeans concentrated a low-cost, high-volume attack on European industry; consumer electronics; and cars. Although the 'new suppliers' have now matured, in many cases other new competitors are emerging using the same techniques.
- Specialty competitors – companies who concentrate on a narrow, often high-volume sector of the market. By using available technology and avoiding the cost of supporting a wide range of products, these companies are winning a significant share of the market and damaging their established competitors' customer base. Examples include book printers, particularly in the high quality 'coffee table' sector; personal computers; and specialty clothes outlets such as ties, socks and jeans.
- Competitors who add value to their products to win volume business, segment markets or who offer packages of products and services that represent better overall value. Examples include insurance companies; computer manufacturers who 'bundle' software with their systems; car manufacturers who include service and rescue packages; and energy companies who include

consultancy and management services in their overall offering.

- Competitors who come from a different discipline but utilise their customer base or their physical location to attack established suppliers. Examples include petrol outlets moving into the convenience store business; banks offering mortgages and insurance services; building societies offering banking services; and management consultancies offering information systems services.

Meeting customer expectations

In many cases, these competitive activities are driven by increasing customer expectations. New car buyers, for example, expect to receive satisfactory service throughout the ownership of the car. The finance package, the after-care programme, the accessories and services such as mobile communications, the convenience of guaranteed rescue services and the benefits of a single source for all motoring services such as bodyshop, repairs, windscreens, spare parts and customisation all put considerable pressure on the resources of a typical local car dealer.

The travelling public expect to buy more than petrol, oil or road-maps when they call at a service station anywhere in the country. To sustain a high quality, consistent retail service across a national network of local outlets changes the nature of fuel station management. Industrial buyers expect a range of support services such as consultancy, implementation and maintenance when they buy capital equipment. Customers who are commissioning complex projects such as new buildings want to simplify their own administration and management tasks by dealing with a small number of suppliers or preferably a single source.

Distributors, retailers and agents expect their suppliers to provide them with a full support package to help them develop their own business. In each of these scenarios, customers expect a standard of service that goes beyond the basic product. The supplier is unlikely to have the skills and resources to provide these additional services without recruiting, retraining or investment. Partnership offers the opportunity to develop these additional services, meet customer expectations and achieve increasingly higher levels of customer satisfaction.

Pressure on costs

Price competition and the need to maintain profitability are increasing pressure on every company to reduce its cost base. Since the recession, companies cannot afford to be complacent about pricing and companies are looking at every aspect of their operations to see where they can reduce costs. In industry, cost reduction not only applies to the cost of bought-in materials and the manufacturing process, it can also be applied to the following areas:

- distribution
- warehousing
- stockholding
- quality control on incoming components
- administering the supply chain
- design and engineering processes
- through-life costs of the product
- operating internal or external support services
- recruiting and training staff
- new product development
- marketing and selling
- achieving customer satisfaction.

As the examples in this chapter have shown, partnership can make an important contribution in each of these areas. Cost reduction is one of the primary reasons behind partnership. In its simplest form, a supplying partner is offered a larger share of the customer's business over a longer period of time in return for agreed price levels maintained over that period of time. The customer then has a better and more predictable cost base, while the supplier enjoys higher levels of business with reduced sales and marketing costs. A more advanced form of partnership sees both companies co-operating on joint cost-reduction exercises, for example by modifying production processes, increasing quality to reduce waste or reworking, or achieving savings through redesign or value engineering of key components.

Rapid technological change

New technology can reduce costs, improve reliability and product performance and increase customer satisfaction. The problem is that technology changes rapidly and few companies have the resources to achieve technical leadership without major investment in research and development and recruitment of high quality technical staff. Increasingly, they rely on the specialised technical expertise of their suppliers to contribute developments in specific areas.

Take a car for example. Technical changes could occur in a large number of unrelated areas, but few of them would be developed by the car manufacturer's own technical staff:

- better tyre design to improve road holding and comfort
- improved seating design to improve comfort and safety

- lighter and stronger materials to reduce overall weight and increase safety
- more sophisticated braking systems to improve safety
- increased use of plastics in non-structural components to reduce overall weight and improve fuel consumption
- development of electronic engine management systems to improve performance, reliability and fuel economy
- improved paint systems to reduce the risk of corrosion and enhance resale values
- introduction of on-board computers on higher-specification models to improve driver convenience
- development of lighting systems to improve safety
- enhancement of audio systems and introduction of mobile communications to improve comfort and convenience
- development of special lubricants to improve vehicle life and reduce overall maintenance costs.

Each one of these technical improvements is likely to come from an external supplier although the impetus may come from the car manufacturer. The car manufacturer would not have the technical resources to achieve industry-best standards in all of these areas, yet, to remain competitive, it must have access to the technology. Partnership with suppliers who have a record of innovation will provide that access. Partnership not only provides access to specialist technology, it may also provide a manufacturer with a specific competitive edge. By developing new products and services that are unique to the partnership, a customer can develop technical advantage over competitors and secure the advantage for a sufficiently long period to build an effective marketing lead.

Competing in a wider market

A chain of estate agents covering south-east England wanted to expand into a national organisation. The cost of setting up new branches would have been prohibitive but, by co-operating with other regional groups who were well managed, the group was able to offer its customers a nationwide service.

A high street chemist wanted to establish a national chain of opticians. Optician departments were already established in a number of larger stores, but to grow the network rapidly, the chemist decided to work in partnership with established local practices. The local practices received administrative and business support and benefited from national branding and advertising, while the chemist obtained an existing practice with an established local customer base.

A national advertising agency was asked by an international client to handle its business across Europe. The agency knew that it would not be able to handle the business effectively without local representation and local market knowledge. If it performed poorly, its business would be threatened by global agencies who had an established international network. It formed a network of associate companies in each of the key territories, selecting partners who shared similar business philosophies and had experience in the client's market.

With the advent of the single European market, transport companies realised that they would have to offer their customers pan-European transport services. By working in partnership with other European transport companies, they were able to offer customers a single source service which simplified administration and reduced costs. By co-operating on a regional basis, the individual transport companies were able to generate higher levels of business and overcome operational problems.

A construction equipment manufacturer knew that customers would depend on a quality service and maintenance facility that would provide a rapid response to local construction sites. Because of the nature of the construction business, with penalty clauses for late completion, equipment downtime was a serious problem. The manufacturer did not have a sufficiently wide distributor network to offer customers a local service across Europe so it set up partnership with local service organisations, providing them with business and technical support, and operating a priority parts delivery service to ensure that they could meet the customers' repair requirements promptly and efficiently.

In each of these examples, the company has been under pressure to extend its operations beyond its own geographical boundaries, either to meet customer requirements, or to compete effectively and achieve targeted growth levels. Growing a network organically would have been a slow and expensive process, but partnership with the right people provides an effective and immediate solution.

Reducing time to market

If we look at the process of new product development, there are a number of important aims:

- to get the product to market in the shortest possible time to gain competitive advantage
- to ensure that the product incorporates the best available solution to meet customer requirements
- to control overall production and development costs to ensure competitive pricing and profitability.

The example of the technical developments in a new car earlier in this chapter demonstrates the value of working in partnership with specialist suppliers to meet the second of these new product aims – ensuring that the product incorporates the best available solution. The same process of partnership can be utilised to reduce overall development time and get the product to market as quickly as possible.

Computer companies, for example, work on a regular series of announcement dates. Quarterly new product announcements enable their customers to plan their own new product development programmes in line with the computer manufacturers, so it is vital that companies can integrate all product development activities within a common time-scale without increasing their own facilities or disrupting their day-to-day activities.

The previous section gave examples of how partnership was used by companies to develop a national or international network of outlets without the lead time needed to set up their own operations. This is one method of using partnership to reduce time to market. In the manufacturing sector, the programme can be divided into smaller critical activities which are then handled by appropriate partners. As well as design and manufacturing processes, the manufacturer can also utilise external partnership services to handle market and customer research, distribution, marketing communications and product launch. Although these services are normally bought in from specialists, the manufacturer has to spend time educating the supplier about the market and the product. By establishing long-term partnerships with specialists, the manufacturer can reduce the learning period and ensure that every aspect of new product development and launch is handled quickly and efficiently.

Dealing with skills shortages

One of the other pressures driving companies is the shortage of skills in key areas such as design, engineering or marketing. Skills shortages mean that staff can be prevented from taking on strategic development tasks because of the pressures of day-to-day working. In companies that have made a large investment in information systems equipment from a number of different sources, there is now a drive to integrate different products so that they operate together and enable companies to improve the competitive advantage they obtain from their investment. Systems integration, however, is just one of the pressures on information systems support staff. They have to train new users, develop new business applications, support and maintain systems and manage relationships with information systems suppliers.

The cost of recruiting and retaining staff of the calibre to handle all of these tasks effectively can be prohibitive and, therefore, outsourcing appears to be the only viable alternative. However, outsourcing without deep involvement in the customer's business can lead to ineffective service, so partnership offers an attractive solution.

Outsourcing can be used to overcome short- and long-term skills shortages and deal with peaks and troughs in the workload. Using the computerisation example again, the implementation of a new departmental system could take a number of months from initial consultation and system development through installation and start-up. Each of the stages would require different skills and different levels of involvement from support staff. The company would have to retain or redeploy staff to meet short-term requirements and this would not represent the best use of resources.

Focus on core skills

Skills shortages are also one of the driving forces behind a company's decision to focus on its core skills. Internal services such as warehousing, facilities management, maintenance, marketing, distribution and research and development can often be handled more efficiently and cost-effectively by external suppliers working in long-term partnership. The focus on core skills does not just apply to departmental or individual activities, it can lead to large diverse groups shedding divisions or companies which do not fit within the core business strategy.

Computer manufacturers, for example, now concentrate on hardware and information systems services. They develop software to run on their systems by working with networks of approved software partners. The software partners may produce standard programs which run on any manufacturer's system, but their partnership programs are specifically designed to take advantage of a particular hardware system. In return the software partners have privileged access to the manufacturer's technical expertise and development plans, and can harmonise their business plans over a long period of time.

The core skills process can also work in another direction. A credit card processing company decided that it had specific skills in high-volume telephone response, transaction processing, mailing and customer account management. These were skills that would be valuable to companies who wished to improve their marketing performance by enhancing those activities, but did not have the resources to carry them out effectively. The credit card company was able to offer its core skills so that partners could concentrate on their core business; as a result, both parties benefited.

A recent approach to improving competitive performance – business process re-engineering – continues many of the activities of core skills development. Re-engineering enables companies to examine the function and contribution of every department and, ultimately, every individual to the overall performance of the organisation. If the individual does not make a significant contribution, their role must be reassessed and they must be trained to improve their performance or redeployed into other strategic activities. Partnership can make an important contribution here by allowing companies to outsource those activities where individuals cannot be retrained or redeployed cost-effectively. This enables the company to develop a more flexible policy and take full advantage of the benefits of re-engineering.

Introduction of new business processes

Re-engineering and core business development are just two of the new business processes that companies are utilising to improve their competitive performance. Total Quality Management, Just-In-Time manufacturing, World Class Manufacturing and many other approaches to business have each provided the manufacturer with a new way to manage the business. Partnership integrates with each of these processes to provide companies with high levels of flexibility and the opportunity to take advantage of advances in manufacturing technology.

Just-In-Time, for example, aims to reduce overall costs by squeezing waste out of the supply system. Manufacturers do not hold buffer stocks, they only hold stocks to meet specific production requirements. Suppliers, in turn, produce sufficient quantities to meet current requirements. The Just-In-Time process depends on high levels of co-operation between manufacturer and supplier, and partnership is the natural business relationship. Information and communications systems which enable partners to exchange product information, plan production and delivery and retrieve information on work-in-progress strengthens the business and physical links between partners. The high levels of co-operation needed to ensure efficient operation by both parties can only operate in a partnership environment.

Total Quality Management, at its logical conclusion, demands integrated quality processes throughout the supply chain, and partnership is often the logical outcome of a drive to improve quality standards. By harmonising quality standards, a manufacturer can reduce the cost of monitoring incoming supplies and ensure quality in his own products.

As this analysis of the forces behind partnership shows, partnership initiatives can come from suppliers or customers, and they can be led by other developments in management practice. At the heart of all the driving forces, however, is the need to improve competitive business performance and, whenever this can be achieved with mutual benefit to both parties, there is a real opportunity for partnership.

SUMMARY

This chapter has introduced the concept of partnership and described why it is important for you to build relationships with your customers to secure long-term business. It has explained how you can co-operate with partners to win business or utilise partnership to add value to your products or services. If you need to improve local marketing performance, partnership could help you achieve that. You can also utilise partnership to develop a joint market or spread the risk in undertaking a major project. One of the most important factors behind partnership is reducing costs. The chapter has shown how you could develop partnership by building links through technology, providing a broader service, or differentiating a service. There are many important factors behind partnership including increasing competition in the market-place, higher customer expectations, pressure on costs, and rapid technological change. Partnership is also important to companies aiming to compete in wider markets, undertaking rapid new product development, or overcoming skills shortages. The introduction of new business processes such as Just-In-Time or core skills development requires partnership in order to succeed.

Self-assessment checklist

- How important is it for you to build relationships with your customers?

- Can you co-operate with partners to win business?

- Can you utilise partnership to add value to your products or services?

- Do you need to improve local marketing performance and how could partnership help you achieve that?

- Could you utilise partnership to develop a joint market?

- Will working with a partner spread the risk in undertaking a major project?

- How could partnership help you reduce costs?

- Could you develop partnership by building links through technology?

- Can partnership help you provide a broader service?

- Will partnership allow you to differentiate a service?

- Do you face increasing competition in the market-place?

- Can partnership help you meet higher customer expectations?

- Do you or your partners face pressure on costs?

- Do your partners have to cope with rapid technological change?

- Are you aiming to compete in wider markets?

- Do you or your partners need to undertake rapid new product development?

- Could partnership help you or your partner overcome skills shortages?

- Will the introduction of new business processes require partnership?

- Are you or your partners focusing on core skills?

22

LIFE CYCLE SERVICES

This chapter describes how the introduction of broad-ranging services enables companies to improve relationships with clients by helping them to improve their business performance throughout a 'life cycle'. While high value professional services such as consultancy provide clients with important strategic benefits, clients may also need longer-term support to effectively implement recommendations and gain real business benefit. Professional services such as training, project management and facilities management have therefore become an important element in providing the client with a 'total business solution'.

Andersen Consulting, for example, introduced services such as facilities management and managed service to complement their traditional information technology consulting activities. In the human resources sector, recruitment consultants, Austin Knight, decided to get more deeply involved with their clients' whole personnel strategy by introducing a range of internal marketing consultancy services to support change management in their clients' organisations.

IDENTIFYING LIFE CYCLE OPPORTUNITIES

One of the most effective ways to identify service opportunities is to look at the problems clients face by analysing a series of business scenarios. Some examples show how the process works:

- Clients need to ensure that they have devised the right strategy to meet their business objectives. They need objective advice and guidance to improve the quality of their own decision making. Practices can meet those requirements by offering consultancy services.
- Clients have identified certain activities which are crucial to their business success. They need help in defining the problems and planning the most appropriate course of action. Consultancy will also be relevant here.
- Clients need to adapt quickly to changing market conditions or competitive threats, but they do not have the resources or skills to succeed. Practices can

offer clients their skills and resources on a project basis so that they can meet short- and long-term requirements.

- Clients need to develop new user and management skills so that they can get the best return from an investment. You can offer your clients training services.

As an example, the drive to improve competitiveness and reduce costs is causing many organisations to investigate the potential of strategies such as Business Process Re-engineering (BPR). Implementing that kind of strategy can have far-reaching consequences and management consultancies have an opportunity to offer their clients a broad range of integrated services including strategy development, business process planning and development, information systems strategy and implementation, change management, training and internal communications.

Another way to identify service opportunities is to look at clients' 'life cycles' – what type of support does a client need at different stages of its 'life' and how can the practice's professional services help them achieve better business performance. The most important stages in the life cycle are described as:

- CONSULT   At this stage, the client's executive team decide on their overall strategy for dealing with key business issues. This is the most important stage for influencing the shape of future policy and the practice should be involved at this stage, particularly if competitors are trying to influence senior decision makers.
- DESIGN   The client has decided the overall strategy and is consulting with individual departments to design specific solutions or incorporate individual requirements into the service specification.
- IMPLEMENT   At this stage, the new service has been introduced and the client concentrates on getting the service up and running as quickly as possible, with minimal disruption to day-to-day operations.
- MANAGE   The manage stage is the equivalent of normal operation. The service has been used successfully and the client's support task is to ensure it continues to be used effectively and delivers business benefits.

As an example, take the introduction of a new computerised accounting system in a small to medium-sized company. The company may be growing rapidly and have no real experience of computerised accounting. An accountancy practice can provide valuable support at each of the four life cycle stages:

Consult

- helping the client to plan an accounting system to meet current and future

needs
- advising on the management and training implications of the new system.

Design

- setting a detailed specification for the system
- advising the client on suitable hardware, software and procedures.

Implement

- providing initial guidance to client staff on using the new system
- recommending or providing training services.

Manage

- reviewing the operation and benefits of the system
- advising on new software to meet changing operating requirements.

It is possible for practices to target their professional services at any stage of the life cycle:

- During the MANAGE stage, the client may not have the capacity or the skills to handle an increasing workload on their own system. The accountancy practice could take over part of the load, working on the client's site or transferring data on to their own systems.
- Although the client may have become an advanced system user, changes in legislative requirements may mean that part of the system is no longer appropriate. The client is actually moving back to the CONSULT stage and may require advice and guidance on adapting to new requirements.

As the example shows, the life cycle is a continuous process and different departments within the same client organisation may be at different stages at the same time.

The life cycle concept can be applied to a number of business scenarios, particularly where clients are introducing new technology or new working practices. The important thing is that clients' needs change at each stage and their own support team may not have the skills or resources to handle all of these tasks cost-effectively. By analysing a client's individual life cycle, a practice can develop a range of services that will provide all the help and guidance that is needed, and will be able to maintain high levels of contact with the client throughout the life cycle.

To make the most effective use of the life cycle approach, the practice needs to develop an understanding of the client's business processes and get to know the skills and resources available. The life cycle provides an opportunity to take over complete services on the clients' behalf or supplement their resources when they need help most.

BENEFITS OF THE PROGRAMME

A life cycle marketing programme is a good basis for developing effective long-term relationships with customers. The life cycle recognises that customers progress through different stages in their utilisation of a programme and this enables the company to identify opportunities to support the customer. This in turn can help to build stronger business relationships and help a company develop a long-term strategy for delivering customer service.

KEY MANAGEMENT TASKS

- Assess your customer's life cycle.
- Identify service opportunities at each stage.
- Compare service requirements with the services you are already delivering.
- Introduce the new services.
- Use the service offering to build stronger relationships with your customers.

SUMMARY

The life cycle is a valuable concept for understanding a customer's business and focusing a service operation on customer's needs. Companies who are already providing customers with specific types of service such as consultancy can use the life cycle concept to identify other opportunities in the four stages of consult, design, implement and manage. The process ensures that customers receive the right level of support at each stage and builds long-term relationships.

Self-assessment checklist

- Do your clients face any of the problems described in the business scenarios?
- How well do you understand the broad business issues and challenges faced by your clients?

- Is new legislation likely to impact on clients' business? How could your services help them overcome potential problems?

- Can you identify the client life cycle that is relevant to the services you provide?

- What stage of the life cycle is your client currently in?

- Would the impact of legislation and technology change the client's position in the life cycle?

- Can you offer your clients professional services that would improve their business performance at current and future life cycle stages?

23

OFFERING CUSTOMERS YOUR SKILLS

This chapter describes how customer services can help you improve relationships with your customers by helping them improve their business performance. Customer services such as installation, training and maintenance have been provided by many companies free as part of an overall package. However, high value services can provide important strategic benefits and they should be included as an integral element of a key account management programme.

MAINTAINING ACCOUNT CONTROL

Look at your customers' buying cycle. How frequently do they make major purchases – monthly, annually, every three years, every five years? The longer the product cycle, the more difficult it is to retain account control. Other companies can be talking to your customers, users may be experiencing problems that you are not aware of, and the decision-making team may be changing in ways that you cannot influence. Loss of contact could mean loss of control.

In the consumer sector, car manufacturers realised that the period between new car sales is the most critical element of customer relations. With customers buying new cars every two to three years on average, sales control is minimal. Manufacturers have therefore focused their efforts on building an effective after-sales operation based on the fact that parts and service operations generate five times the number of customer contacts as new car sales. The manufacturers realised that they had been losing both repair and scheduled maintenance work to 'fast-fit' operations. This meant a loss of revenue to their dealerships, but also denied them the opportunity to maintain customer satisfaction between car purchases.

The same principle can be applied to the information technology market where new system sales have similar purchase lead times of several years. Computer manufacturers had been losing maintenance business to independent service companies; they also found that the customers' information systems strategy and choice of systems was being driven, not by the manufacturers, but by management consultancies. When management consultancies moved into other areas of information systems service such as application development and managed service and, when independent service companies expanded their activities, the computer manufacturers lost even more account control.

Although service companies and management consultancies were not the manufacturers' direct competitors, they were enjoying high levels of contact with key decision makers at senior and middle management level, and this influenced future business opportunities. By introducing a broad range of customer services, the manufacturers would be able to build high levels of contact with decision makers throughout the customer organisation.

IMPROVING LOYALTY AND CONTACT

As the previous section mentioned, customer contact is one of the most important benefits of a customer service programme. If we take the example of the computer manufacturer, we can identify a number of stages where customer service can be used to increase the frequency and quality of customer contact:

- strategic consultancy – helping the customer develop an information systems strategy in line with corporate objectives. This brings the company into contact with the senior executive team and provides valuable information on the customer's future business plans;
- information systems consultancy – turning the strategy into a practical solution. This provides contact opportunities at senior executive and operational levels;
- implementation services – helping the customer to install and introduce a new system without recruiting specialist staff or overloading his own support staff. This helps to ensure that the customer's system is implemented effectively, increasing customer satisfaction and loyalty;
- training services – providing the customer with skills development. This builds useful contact with departmental managers and users;
- managed services – which cover a wide range of maintenance and systems management activities. This provides the supplier with one of the best opportunities for continuous contact with information systems staff and gives the supplier a valuable insight into the customer's changing systems needs.

There are many other services that could be included on this list, but they demonstrate the principle of improved contact. These services also make an important contribution to the success of a customer's business and that, in turn, can improve customer loyalty. If a customer was to provide these services internally, it would put considerable pressure on his or her own resources or prevent him or her achieving the full benefits of his investment in the new system. Customers therefore become dependent on your services for the efficient running of their own operations and this can help to strengthen relationships.

IDENTIFYING SERVICE OPPORTUNITIES

One of the most effective ways to identify service opportunities is to look at the problems your customers face by analysing a series of business scenarios. Some examples show how the process works:

- Your customers need to ensure that they have devised the right strategy to meet their business objectives. They need objective advice and guidance to improve the quality of their own decision making. You could meet those requirements by offering consultancy services.
- Your customers have identified certain activities which are crucial to their business success. They need help in defining the problems and planning the most appropriate course of action. Consultancy will also be relevant here.
- Your customers need to adapt quickly to changing market conditions or competitive threats, but they do not have the resources or skills to succeed. You can offer your customers your skills and resources on a project basis so that they can overcome short- and long-term requirements.
- Your customers need to develop new user and management skills so that they can get the best return from the products and services they have bought from you. You can offer your customers training services.
- Your customers need to ensure that their products are continually operational and providing the business benefits they were designed for. By offering your customers maintenance services or managing their equipment for them, you can ensure that their products are kept in the best possible condition.

These business scenarios help you to identify opportunities for offering services to your customers. Customers may provide many of these services from their own resources, but it is possible to get further involved through the growth in outsourcing.

OUTSOURCING

Outsourcing is a growing trend in companies seeking to concentrate on their core business, rather than attempting to do everything themselves. By using outside specialists to handle activities such as maintenance, systems management, distribution, fleet management and customer support, companies can make better use of their own resources and benefit from a quality, cost-effective service from suppliers who specialise in the activity. Outsourcing provides an opportunity to build closer relations with your key account customers by offering them vital services.

DELIVERING THE CUSTOMER SERVICES

The next part of this chapter looks at a number of customer services in more detail to help you understand the requirements and implications of providing these services.

Consultancy

As the earlier part of this chapter showed, consultancy services can help your customers to determine the right product strategy to meet their business objectives. By working at this stage with a senior executive team, you can ensure that your products get the right assessment and that senior executives understand your business and your strategic skills.

However, one of the main problems facing the consultant who is also a vendor is the risk of bias. Customers like their consultants to offer independent advice free from any product ties. Your consultancy service must therefore be clearly separated from your sales activities and you must ensure that you have consultants with the breadth of experience to deliver objective advice that adds value to a relationship. One advantage that 'vendor consultants' have is that they have practical experience of the industry and the technology they are working with and they can therefore recommend realistic solutions that will work.

In selecting consultants, customers look for broad industry experience and a track record of successful projects. You may need to recruit consultants from outside your company to ensure that you have people with the status and experience to deal confidently with your customer's senior management team. Members of your salesforce or your technical team are unlikely to have the breadth of experience or the ability to deal with strategic issues at boardroom level.

To support your direct consultancy activities, you may find it useful to run other background/briefing activities such as:

- industry seminars organised by your company, featuring speakers from a wide variety of organisations, which demonstrate that you are aware of the strategic issues facing your customers and supporting their whole business
- management reports and guides to strategic issues which demonstrate that

you are capable of working at boardroom level

● executive briefing centres, purpose-built meeting areas where your customers' senior management teams can spend time away from day-to-day pressures discussing the strategic issues that surround the introduction and management of your products in relation to their business objectives

● publication of 'consultancy' articles in management publications read by senior decision makers.

Activities like these help to position your company as a strategic supplier and give credibility to your consultancy services.

Introducing consultancy services provides you with a number of important benefits in key account management. These include:

● ensuring that you are in a position to influence senior executives

● providing you with an understanding of the strategic business issues facing your customers now and in the future

● allowing you to influence your customers' decision-making process at an early stage

● positioning your company as a strategic supplier.

Technical support

Technical support is one of the most common types of customer service and it can take many forms:

● technical advisory service
● design and application service
● field technical support
● installation.

Technical support is vital if your company is supplying components or technical products and services. Your technical support can help your customers to improve the performance of their products and make them more competitive in their own markets. By working closely with the customer design team, you can ensure that your company becomes a preferred supplier for new products. Involvement in the product development phase enables your team to get a better feel for your customers' product plans and technical problems that you can overcome.

A high level of technical service is essential if your company supplies complex products or services or if your customers are developing new products, but technical service can also help to differentiate commodity products and basic components. A bearing manufacturer supplying transmission bearings worked closely with an equipment manufacturer to rationalise the design of a new product through value engineering. By substituting a transmission bearing with integral housing, sealing and lubrication facility for a series of separate components, the manufacturer was able to reduce machining and assembly costs. The bearing supplier was able to put considerable distance between his added-value engineering solution and a standard component, and overcome price comparisons. The company was also able to build closer working relationships with the design department and to build future modifications and product developments into the customer's forward plans.

Project management

Project management services help customers to take on or complete projects for which they do not have the skills or resources. By using your skilled staff, they can have the project carried out by experienced specialists and they do not have to recruit new staff or retrain their own. Projects can be long term or short term and might include:

- installing new products or systems
- helping to redesign a product
- carrying out specialist services or maintenance work
- introducing a new departmental or corporate operating procedure.

The customer may need support because his or her own staff are overloaded or because he or she wants them to concentrate on core business activities. To encourage customers to use your project services, you may need to explain the hidden cost benefits of using outside specialists:

- The customer can respond to threats or opportunities quickly.
- The customer can introduce new business processes quickly without disrupting day-to-day activities.
- Projects will be carried out to the highest standards by specialists.
- Projects will be completed within an agreed time-scale without recruiting staff or diverting internal staff.
- Projects will be handled cost-effectively compared with internal resources.

Management consultancies use project services to implement their strategic recommendations and retain control over the account. They are aware that customers may not understand the full management implications of fundamental changes and, therefore, may fail to achieve the full business benefit. If the management team feel disappointed with the results, they may blame the consultancy. It is important to the consultancy's long-term business prospects that their recommendations are properly implemented so project services play a vital role.

Training services

Training services help your customers make the most effective use of the products they buy from you or provide them with additional skills to improve their business performance. In the computer industry, for example, training is offered at a number of different levels:

- senior executive courses in planning and managing information systems. The training programmes help executives relate their information systems to their corporate objectives and ensure that they select the correct system. This type of training helps improve the quality of decision making and demonstrates that the supplier is helping the customer to improve business performance;
- courses for departmental managers in using information systems. The training programmes help departmental managers understand how information systems will impact on their day-to-day operations and provides them with guidelines on managing their systems. This type of training builds understanding and overcomes any potential resistance in the decision-making team;
- courses for information systems specialists. This type of training improves specialists' skills and keeps them up to date with the suppliers' latest technical developments;
- courses for operators and users. This is the traditional type of training included in a product/service package. It is an essential element, ensuring that the product is used correctly;
- courses for systems support staff. This type of training helps reduce the service load on the supplier. By ensuring that customers' internal support staff can deal with day-to-day queries and system management, the supplier can use his support specialists to deliver higher value services.

The training can be delivered in a number of ways:

- using an internal training department and employing training specialists at a central site
- delivering training services at the customer's site using your own training specialists
- using an independent training organisation to deliver training
- developing distance learning packages or publishing training material for use by the customer's own training specialists.

Training services add value to the account relationship by improving the customer's overall business performance. They should be an integral part of your key account programme if the following conditions apply:

- your products are technically complex
- the introduction of your product will bring about fundamental change in the customer's organisation
- your customers do not have the product experience to make effective purchasing decisions
- your technology changes rapidly.

Maintenance and facilities management services

Although few companies would overlook product maintenance as an integral element of their product/service package, the method of delivering maintenance can improve account control:

- To overcome the threats from independent maintenance companies, suppliers are developing more sophisticated, quality-controlled maintenance services. They invest in service tools specially tailored to their products or set up service databases which enable rapid fault diagnosis or preventative maintenance.
- Suppliers offer their customers different levels of service, for example gold, silver or bronze standard. These options which include differences in level of cover, response time, spares holding and cost can be fine-tuned to provide customers with a tailored service that matches their support requirements.
- Managed service, where a supplier takes over complete responsibility for managing all service activities on site equipment is a valuable approach when customers have bought equipment from a number of different suppliers and have to co-ordinate different service suppliers. The managed service provider liaises with the other manufacturers' service departments, co-ordinates their activities, imposes quality standards and provides the customer with a single invoice. The customer benefits from more consistent standards of service and simpler administration, while the supplier increases account control and reduces competitive threats.
- Facilities management where a supplier takes over the complete management and maintenance of a customer's equipment is more appropriate than managed service where the customer's equipment is predominately supplied by one manufacturer. As part of the facilities management contract, the manufacturer upgrades the equipment so that it always reflects the latest product development. The customer does not have to provide any support staff so is free to concentrate on core business activities.

This type of service is a long way from the 'fix it when it goes wrong' approach and it demonstrates how maintenance can deliver powerful customer benefits. It not only ensures that the customer's equipment is kept in the best condition, it can reduce the burden of service administration and free service staff for more productive tasks.

Service standards

The section on maintenance demonstrated how superior service standards can differentiate a supplier from an independent service company. It is important that you position your company as a quality service supplier. Your customers will assess your performance according to a number of factors:

- adherence to an independent quality standard such as BS 5750
- your service response mechanism – how quickly and easily can customers contact you when they have a query or a problem
- your service infrastructure – spares level, service network, location and number of service specialists, investment in service tools
- your capability for managed service – training, management resources, administrative support and ability to co-ordinate other specialists
- your service performance – response times, success rate, your measurement of customer satisfaction and your escalation procedures for problems that cannot be resolved.

If you are serious about using customer services to improve account control, you need to ensure that you can provide a specialist quality service that enhances your corporate reputation. The importance of customer services has led many suppliers to reposition themselves as 'total solutions' companies providing, not just products, but all the supporting services that will enable their customers to achieve full business benefit from their investment in the product.

Using third party service delivery

You may not have the skills or resources to operate this level of service support to your key account customers. It may be possible to work in partnership with a specialist service company to provide the right level of support. In selecting a service partner, you should carefully assess their contribution:

- Do they understand your products?
- Can they provide the right level of cover to your customers?
- Can you control their service delivery through quality standards?
- Are they investing in the development of their own service standards?
- Do they represent any form of competitive threat to your account control?

Provided independent service partners meet these requirements, they can provide you with a ready-made service solution without an investment in your own resources.

SELLING SERVICES

Services can be a major contributor to account control and may increase revenue and profit. However, there are a number of obstacles to overcome in selling services:

- You may have supplied certain services free of charge as part of an overall package. You now need to persuade your customers that they should pay for those services. You need to explain how chargeable services add value and help the customer improve business performance.
- Your customers may not realise that they need certain services. You have to explain the business benefits and the hidden cost benefits of support services. Relating your services to the customer's business scenarios improves understanding.
- Your salesforce may be reluctant to sell services because they are low in value compared with capital products. You must stress the account control benefits of service support and encourage the salesforce to invest time for long-term benefit.

SUMMARY

Services make a major contribution to account control by increasing the frequency of contact between product purchase and helping your customers improve their business performance. As well as increasing contact, they also represent an opportunity to increase revenue and profitability. To identify service opportunities, you should assess business scenarios faced by your customers – what problems can your services overcome? Many companies who provided their own support services internally are now outsourcing to reduce costs and increase flexibility and this provides a further opportunity to build the customer's dependence on your services. Consultancy, technical support, project management, training, and maintenance services are among the most important services and they contribute in different ways to key account control and development. If you are providing a 'total solution' to your customers, you must ensure that all the services are delivered to a consistent quality standard. Alternatively, you can work with a service partner, provided the partner can meet your quality standards.

Self-assessment checklist

- Does your customer purchasing cycle make a service strategy important?

- How frequently do you contact your customers?

- How could services increase that contact?

- Would services make your customers more dependent on you?

- Can you calculate the potential revenue from services? Would it make a significant contribution to the bottom line?

- What problems do your customers face that your services could overcome?

- What services do your customers already carry out internally?

- Would outsourcing help them to reduce their own support costs?

- What type of consultancy services can you offer your customers? Do you have staff of 'consultant' calibre who can succeed at boardroom level?

- How can you improve levels of technical support?

- Can you identify 'projects' that will benefit your customers' business?

- How would different types of training service contribute to your customer's overall business development?

- How can you develop your current maintenance services to improve account control?

- Are you able to deliver quality service internally or would it be better to work with a service partner?

- How do you plan to sell services?

24

CONSISTENT SERVICE NATIONWIDE

'The problem is that each of the outlets perform at a different level. I want every customer who buys from one of our branches to know immediately that they are in a . . .' When a company can say that about its local network, it has achieved consistency. The quotation underlines the problems that companies marketing through multiple outlets face – how to provide customers with consistent standards of service. Many commentators argue that it doesn't matter because customers are unlikely to visit more than one outlet, so they will not be making comparisons. The key issue is how to attract prospects to an outlet in the first place and turn them into customers.

Advertising that says 'you'll find more choice at our supermarket or enjoy better service at our fast food outlet' is delivering a promise that every outlet bearing the name will offer a certain level of quality. If the outlet does not deliver that promise the customer will be disappointed and will not return again. There are also certain types of retail outlet where customers are likely to visit a number of different locations – hotels, petrol stations, banks, restaurant chains and airlines. Customers do have a choice when they are on the move and they will use their experience of the local outlet to judge other locations. While companies may not be able to achieve consistency in every aspect – size of outlet, number of staff, stock levels – these may not be crucial factors. What they must try to control are the factors that influence customer satisfaction – the quality of customer service. A London resident, on holiday, using a small village bank branch would not expect the same number of service points, the same range of products and services, or even the same opening hours as their main branch, but they would have certain expectations about the type and quality of service they were given.

WHEN CONSISTENT LOCAL SERVICE IS IMPORTANT

Consistent local service is important to companies who market their products through local outlets:

- companies who market through independent retailers
- companies with a franchised distributor network
- companies with a network of local branches.

BRANDING LOCAL OUTLETS

This ability to reproduce consistent standards in every outlet is integral to branding. Customers know what to expect from a Holiday Inn, a Pizza Hut, a BP service station, Habitat store, Martin the Newsagent or Boots the Chemist – each of these outlets has a set of brand values built up over a long period of time in the same way as branded products such as Kellogs, Cadbury, BMW, Marks and Spencer, P&O, Black & Decker. Customers immediately assume that the product must be good because a brand leader would not market a poor product.

Using branding to grow a new network

By applying the same approach to retail outlets and branches, companies hope to achieve the same levels of customer awareness. During the 1980s, financial institutions used the branding approach to build up networks of estate agents to take full advantage of the current property boom. Small regional networks and independent agents became branches of such organisations as Prudential Properties, Black Horse Agencies and many others. The people and the offices were the same, but the branches now had the backing and support of a major company with access to a nationwide information network and the benefits of integrated management practices. The fact that the housing market collapsed at the end of the 1980s led many companies to withdraw from this type of operation but that should not reflect on the potential long-term benefits of this type of operation.

The same process is in operation in the optician trade where companies such as Boots have taken over a network of independent local practices to set up a nationwide chain of Boots' Opticians. In some larger Boots outlets, there were already optician departments within the store, but, in smaller towns, separate outlets have been used to build up the national network. Once again the people and the outlets are the same, but customers now have greater choice, better prices in some cases, and confidence in a brand name. Boots support the outlet with the backing of advertising, management systems and training. The independent outlets benefit from the higher profile, the Boots brand name and the value of Boots national advertising campaigns to attract higher levels of business.

Branding franchised services

Dairy Crest, the milk distributors, have recently changed the basis of their milk delivery system to try to improve the quality of their service and improve their own brand performance. They had previously employed their own roundsmen and managed the business directly. They switched in 1992 to a new basis – franchised roundsmen – where each roundsman was responsible for building his own business. Dairy Crest provided business support, training and the vehicle together with administrative support and a selection of promotions and campaigns in which the roundsman could participate. The roundsman was responsible for efficient delivery and collection and could boost his own turnover and profit by selling more milk or selling additional products.

By switching to a franchise agreement, Dairy Crest immediately acquired a committed workforce who should, in theory, boost the group's overall turnover and profit. They also retained an efficient local delivery service at a time when there was an apparent decline in the availability of doorstep services in the wake of increased sales through supermarkets and other convenience outlets. The Dairy Council had already been running a series of television commercials reinforcing the benefits of doorstep delivery. Dairy Crest were able to introduce customer service standards as part of the franchise agreement so that they could also control the quality and consistency of the service.

Consistency and quality of service are crucial to the long-term branding of retail outlets and the key to their achievement is quality standards and the availability of training to achieve those standards.

QUALITY STANDARDS

Chapter 6, Setting customer focus standards, outlines the key requirements to deliver a quality service to customers. The requirements are qualitative rather than quantitive but these can be translated into measurable targets which local outlets must achieve. This extract from a customer focus manual shows how the process works:

> Branches must conform with our customer focus standards and should achieve the following targets:

- train ** staff from the following departments to achieve quality standards
- maintain adequate stock cover for £** volume turnover
- maintain a fleet of delivery vehicles to reach ** customers
- provide ** square metres of selling space with adequate trained staff to serve ** customers per hour at peak hours

- respond to written enquiries within ** days
- keep queue waiting times to ** minutes
- respond to telephone enquiries within ** minutes
- aim at delivery within ** hours of order
- deal with customer queries within ** hours
- escalate any serious queries that cannot be resolved within ** hours
- make customer care visits to top ten customers at least once a month
- visit all customers within a three-month period.

SKILLS PROFILE

Performance reviews and customer surveys provide the starting-point for developing the skills needed to deliver the highest standard of quality and customer service at each outlet. Performance improvement programmes can be *ad hoc* activities designed to improve performance in specific areas or they can be incorporated into branch business development programmes which are designed to improve overall business performance.

The marketing plan should incorporate a skills profile for all the staff who will be involved in meeting the local outlet's business objectives and this provides a basis for planning local training requirements. The profile should be developed by the local manager working in conjunction with a training specialist from the head office team or from an independent training organisation. The skills profile will detail the number of people required to deliver the various services at branch level and identify the skills they need to provide an efficient professional service. The profile should also assess the experience of key people within the outlet to identify promotion prospects and evaluate the level of management and supervisory skills available.

This skills profile ensures that the training programme can be tailored to the needs of different outlets and individuals within the outlets. A tailored training programme is more likely to provide the outlet with the right skills to meet its business objectives than is an all-purpose training programme which does not recognise differences between local markets. The skills profile and the training plan that is based on it can be used as the basis for a training management database which will ensure that each outlet receives the right training services and the right training information.

The Speedwing Training survey has already been mentioned in earlier chapters. Speedwing Training is the training division of British Airways, originally established to carry out the massive training exercise which British Airways undertook to build its customer service skills before privatisation. The division now uses its customer service training skills and its specialist travel industry knowledge to deliver standard and customised training to companies in the travel business as well as other companies who depend on high standards of customer service. Travel agents represent a high proportion of Speedwing's customer base and, to help agents improve their local marketing performance, Speedwing developed a training partnership programme.

They prepared a questionnaire which helped the travel agents identify the skills within their own organisation. Each type of job was assessed from director or general manager, through supervisors, sales staff, customer representatives and business or package holiday specialists. Each member of staff detailed their experience and their qualifications to date. The agency also provided a profile of its business – whether it concentrated on business or holiday travel, or whether it offered specialist services in any particular area.

The profile, together with information on numbers of staff and turnover of the agency enabled Speedwing to build a training/skills profile which was used to develop individual training road-maps. The agency appointed a training co-ordinator who was responsible for gathering the information to develop the original profile and who would liaise with Speedwing to implement the new training programme. Speedwing were able to use the information in the database to develop a customised training plan for each travel agency branch and to mail training information that was relevant to each branch's needs. This overcame the problem of travel agencies receiving large volumes of information that might not be relevant to their needs. It also enabled Speedwing to build a training partnership with the travel agencies and use that partnership to improve the quality of service available to British Airways customers.

COMMUNICATING TRAINING

Working with local outlets to identify their training needs and tailor courses to their requirements is an essential stage in making the best use of local skills; however, it is also important to communicate the scope and importance of training to local outlets to ensure that they participate in training programmes. Communications should be aimed at

- the senior manager
- departmental manager
- trainees
- training specialist.

Senior managers

Since it is the senior managers within local outlets who control the funds available for training, training should be positioned as an essential investment in the future success and profitability of the organisation. Training is not perceived as a current expense but as a long-term business investment. It is also an investment which will result in improved customer service and better staff relations – intangibles which make a major contribution to the business, but are not easily quantified. It is important to stress how skills development helps to improve the local outlet's competitive ability and provides it with a clear growth path to meet future business objectives and deal with rapid changes in the market-place. Senior managers in the local outlet do not need to know the details of training programmes, they need to understand the contribution they will make to the business.

Departmental managers

Departmental managers are under increasing pressure to produce better and better results or to increase output and production with fewer and fewer resources. Training can help to improve staff performance and help to relieve some of those pressures. However the training must be seen as relevant and it must be positioned as helping to overcome day-to-day problems. Training should also be convenient and practical. Although most departmental managers understand the long-term benefits of training, they may be loathe to release key staff for periods of time when they are under pressure to achieve results. The training proposals must be convenient, not time-consuming and promise improved practical results which will lead to short- and long-term departmental improvements.

Trainees

Trainees need to know that they play a vital role within the organisation and that their contribution is valued. Training will help to improve their personal skills and ensure that they can continue to make an increasing contribution and deal confidently with the problems of an increasingly complex, rapidly changing market. Trainees also need to understand why their skills need to be improved and how the new skills will help them improve service to customers. By demonstrating the change in customer needs through surveys and customer comments, the company can demonstrate what customers expect and want from staff at every level.

Training specialists

Training specialists within local outlets also need to be kept up to date with training developments; they are responsible for identifying training needs and organising the courses. The supplier's training programme should be positioned as a valuable addition to the resources they have available.

TRAINING OPTIONS

Convenience and relevance were identified as key messages to trainees and their managers. There is a pressure on time and funds which can act as a barrier to an effective programme of local training. Suppliers should therefore look carefully at the way they deliver training so that they can provide the greatest benefits with the least inconvenience.

There are a number of options:

- Companies with large branch or distributor networks may run central training centres for technical, management or sales training.
- Local or distance learning options may improve the reach and effectiveness of the training budgets.
- Video has been used as a support or substitute for face-to-face training. While there are many excellent general-purpose training videos, they lack the specific content and the ability to be tailored to local needs.
- Corporate video and television networks can be used to relay information around an organisation and provide a tailored information in very sophisticated networks. Although their primary role is to improve internal communications and provide up-to-date management information in a convenient format, the networks can also be used to broadcast training material, product information and market information which can be integrated with a branch training programme.
- Interactive video takes video a stage nearer to personalised training by providing a training resource which can be tailored to an individual's own rate of progress.
- Companies who do not have the funds to invest in sophisticated training technology have also used correspondence courses to train staff who are too far from training centres to take advantage of the facilities.

RHP Bearings, an international engineering company with a worldwide distributor network, used a correspondence course produced in ten languages to improve product and application knowledge among distributor sales and service staff. The course, which consists of 30 separate modules, was extremely popular and was adopted by a number of international engineering colleges as a basic course for residential students. Although correspondence courses may seem extremely basic in relation to other training techniques, they have been proved extremely effective and they may form a growing part of the return to self-study methods.

Recent developments in management training indicate that self-study will become increasingly important. The National Vocational Qualification (NVQ) programme, which seeks to improve the competence of middle and junior managers uses an integrated set of practical, on-the-job training, short workshops, workbooks and reference books to enable managers to improve their competence against a range of disciplines needed for success in general management. Managers follow a series of courses which develop core skills and which are directly related to the tasks they carry out. NVQs can be used to develop general management competence within the local network and can complement the more specific market-based training offered by training specialists.

Many organisations, conscious of the problems their branches face in releasing staff to go on courses, are taking training to the branches. ICL, for example, operated a programme called the SkillsVan which transported training resources around the country to different ICL branches and contained all the material needed to operate a wide range of training programmes.

Ford ran a Dealer Training service which developed and delivered customised training courses for individual dealerships. The programme consisted of a training assessment followed by a review of training needs and a specified number of days' training per month to enhance key skills within the dealership. These training options are helping to make training more convenient within the branch and raise the standards of customer service throughout a branch network.

CONCENTRATING RESOURCES IN CENTRES OF EXCELLENCE

An alternative to running large-scale local training programmes is to take certain highly skilled tasks out of the local outlet and move them into centres of excellence. These are most likely to be tasks that require scarce skills that are not available in every branch. By putting together skilled people in centres of excellence and making them available to customers throughout the country, a supplier can offer a consistent level of service everywhere.

Earlier in this book, we discussed the role of the ICL Customer Reception Centre in improving the quality of response to customer queries. The Customer Reception Centre was part of an overall strategy which included the development of centres of excellence and the introduction of sophisticated service tools and databases. Hand-held terminals, for example, are now used in a number of different industries to carry out service diagnosis and to retrieve and access service information. Service engineers can key in fault symptoms and compare the problems they have found with known faults recorded on the service database. They also use the terminals to log details of a current fault so that the main service database can be updated. Tools like this ensure that locally based service engineers can deliver an increasingly consistent standard of service without investing in major training programmes.

UTILISING BEST PRACTICE

To help build team spirit within a local network and to improve overall performance and consistency, suppliers are encouraging their outlets to participate in developing standards by sharing examples of best practice. In an earlier chapter, we gave the example of Johnson Controls, an international components manufacturer, who utilised international teams to help develop the best possible solution when they were opening a new plant. Teams from plants in other territories would work together to identify opportunities to use best practice in the new plant and also to highlight any potential risks.

The Arlington Motor Company used a similar method to introduce consistent standards into a disparate group of car dealerships. They realised that the performance of individual outlets was, to a certain extent, determined by the skills and attitudes of the dealer principal. The head office team identified the critical performance factors and established benchmarks for each factor. However, rather than impose common standards on the local outlets, the head office team decided to introduce change through participation.

They identified 'star performers' within the network, and invited them to a hotel to work for a week with an independent consultant and share their experiences. By the end of the week, the group had prepared a proposal for best practice within each of the group's operating activities – car sales, commercial vehicles, leasing, parts, service and fleet business. The draft proposals were circulated to management teams within each outlet for comment and suggestion and the result was a set of group operating standards which were acceptable throughout the network. By concentrating on the most important factors and achieving a high level of participation, the group was able to deal with the problem of 'performance scatter' in a large, semi-independent network.

ACHIEVING CONSISTENT VISUAL STANDARDS

It is not only quality standards that need to be consistent. Visual identity is a critical element in signalling to customers and the local network that the company means business, and a new corporate identity is an opportunity to introduce new standards of performance. Corporate identity is the term given to the visual appearance of a company. It includes:

- the colours
- the company logo
- typeface
- uniforms
- appearance of retail outlets
- visual standards imposed on brochures, advertisements and other communications material.

A corporate identity should ideally reflect what the company stands for in terms of quality and direction. A good corporate identity is timeless and is carefully guarded by its owners. Over a period of time, the corporate identities of organisations like IBM, Shell, BP and Ford have evolved in minute detail, but are clearly related to the original identity. The identities of organisations like British Telecom and British Airways, on the other hand, have changed more radically to reflect new corporate values and directions. Both sets of identities have succeeded in achieving an important communications task for their owners and both have helped to build a reputation for excellence and achievement.

Companies maintain the strength of their identity by implementing it across every form of visual communication and ensuring that the identity is used consistently on every occasion. It is particularly important for organisations whose activities are diverse or geographically spread that their total strength should be recognised. This also gives the constituent units within a large organisation a sense of belonging to a team.

Corporate identity is therefore an essential element in local marketing support. It provides the opportunity to impose a consistent appearance on each outlet in the network so that customers immediately recognise the outlet, and it enables a brand identity to be built around the network.

Consistent appearance

The most important aspect of corporate identity is that it imposes a consistent visual appearance and standard on each outlet and ensures that the corporate reputation is communicated effectively. Corporate identity does not just impose consistency for the sake of consistency, the corporate standards have been carefully designed to reflect customers' needs and the quality of service available. When George Davis and the David Davis consultancy developed the original identity for the Next retail chain, the identity was designed to reflect a certain consumer lifestyle and to provide an efficient, cost-effective method of displaying the company's merchandise.

Travellers on the move are attracted by the competing signage of BP, Shell, Esso, Gulf, Fina and a host of other national and regional petrol companies. By linking a strong corporate identity to high standards of customer service, any one of these signs should ensure that the customers will immediately be aware of the whole service on offer. The use of corporate identity has become even more complicated now that petrol stations have been transformed into roadside retail outlets catering for motorists and local residents. The identity of a petrol station no longer signals just the name of a company, but the promise of a certain standard of service.

Consistency is more important when the outlets are not part of a franchised network, but are independent outlets who may be operating multiple franchises. Although it is difficult to impose an overall identity on an outlet like this, the use of selected elements such as signage or the use of corporate colours or a logo on the building or on distributor communications material can help to maintain levels of recognition and ensure that customers understand the benefits of dealing with that outlet.

LAUNCHING A NEW IDENTITY

The introduction of a new identity does not just depend on successful implementation, it takes an effective launch to the local network to ensure that they accept it and understand their role in the transfer. The launch can be handled in a number of ways:

- by holding a national launch event attended by key people from the local network. They are given a presentation on the new identity and practical guidelines on its implementation.
- local outlets receive a launch guide which provides a full explanation of the changes, together with the procedures for implementation.
- a presentation at the individual outlet to explain the detailed implementation of the programme.

If the presentation is not handled effectively, the local outlets will not give the programme their full commitment, and they may not carry out all the critical activities that ensure success.

Introducing the identity to local staff

It is not sufficient to impose a new identity on a local network without explanation and without ensuring that staff understand the implications for organisational performance. Corporate identity must be accompanied by the highest standards of customer care and by remedial action in other areas of corporate weakness if it is to derive the greatest benefit from the new identity. A new identity is an opportunity for staff to reassess the standards they offer and it provides visible evidence of their commitment to change.

Part of the identity implementation process must therefore be a training programme which explains what the new identity is supposed to convey and how that converts to practical actions in the local outlet. For example, if the identity conveys an innovative, market-focused organisation that is dedicated to the highest standards of customer care, it is vital that staff actually achieve this. Poor customer service, old-fashioned methods of business and administrative efficiency can ruin the effect of any identity.

When Case Europe introduced a new retail-led identity into their European parts network, they wanted to convert the network from local warehouses to proactive market-led retail centres which would succeed through quality of service. As well as developing a new merchandising system and a new signage system, they introduced a new range of fast-moving products that would be suitable for a self-service outlet. To ensure that local staff would be able to take advantage of the new opportunities, the company ran courses on retail techniques which included product display, stockholding, customer service and merchandising.

SUMMARY

This chapter has described one of the major problems faced by companies marketing through multiple outlets – how to ensure that customers receive the same standard of service in every branch. It shows how consistency can be used as the basis for branding local outlets in the same way as products. The chapter has described how quality standards such as BS 5750 are increasingly used at local level to measure and monitor performance in line with agreed standards. Staff skills are a key element of consistent performance and the chapter has shown how local skills profiles are used to develop targeted training programmes. It is essential to communicate the benefits of training to local management and staff and to offer them flexible training options. The chapter has provided examples of this and shown how some organisations deal with the problem of performance scatter by concentrating resources in centres of excellence or by utilising best practice from around their networks. The second part of the chapter explains the importance of consistent visual standards, explaining the scope of corporate identity programmes and showing how they reflect changing standards of customer care.

Self-assessment checklist

- How important is consistency to your network?
- Do you brand your network in the same way as your products?
- What are the brand values of your network and how well do they reflect customer expectations?
- Is it important that you transfer existing brand values to new outlets?
- Can you apply measurable quality standards to your network?
- Which processes would you apply quality to?
- Can you apply international quality standards to your local outlets?
- Is it practicable to register your network under an independent quality scheme?
- How do you measure your local customers' views of quality?
- Do you utilise customer response to improve quality standards?
- Do your local outlets understand the importance of training and do they have effective training programmes in position?
- Which skills are crucial to consistent performance throughout your network?
- Can you utilise different training options to ensure that the critical skills are developed?
- Could you take certain skilled critical activities out of local outlets into centres of excellence?
- Are you encouraging your outlets to share best practice with the rest of the network?
- Do you have a strong corporate identity and is it used consistently throughout the network?

- Have you evaluated local customer perceptions of your corporate identity and do they reflect the right values?

- Is the strength of your corporate identity being eroded by inconsistent local use?

- Can you control the use of the corporate identity more effectively?

25

RECOGNISING CUSTOMER SATISFACTION

Customer service is a business process that can be managed and measured. It ensures that the company can retain customers and ensure future income and profitability. In terms of customer care performance, the customer satisfaction index is the most efficient method of measuring achievement and improvement. A customer satisfaction index takes the results from a number of satisfaction surveys and allocates a numerical value to key customer satisfaction indicators. A department, company or local outlet is then given an overall index of performance which can be compared with other groups and measured on a year-on-year basis. Customer satisfaction ratings are a direct method of assessing customer care performance and they provide a means for motivating staff to improve customer care standards.

WHEN CUSTOMER SATISFACTION RATINGS ARE IMPORTANT

Customer satisfaction ratings are an important vehicle for measuring comparative performance. They are valuable in the following scenarios:

- when different groups need to be compared
- when it is important to encourage increasingly higher levels of customer satisfaction
- as a means of motivating staff to greater performance
- as a means of involving customers in the process of service measurement.

DEVELOPING CUSTOMER SATISFACTION SURVEYS

The basis of customer satisfaction ratings is a customer satisfaction survey. This is sent to customers who have purchased a product or service at intervals, a week or a month after purchase, for example, and six months or a year after initial purchase. The first questionnaire is to establish the customers' response to the way the sale was handled, and the second to establish how the customer feels about the product or service in use and how they feel about the after-care they have received from the outlet. The questionnaire asks customers to respond to questions with a scale of satisfaction – fully satisfied, very satisfied, satisfied, not very satisfied, very dissatisfied – or alternatively asked to respond on a numerical scale, 'on a scale of 1-10, how satisfied were you with . . . 1 is very dissatisfied, 10 is very satisfied'. Customers can also provide written comments on aspects of the service and, in some cases, ask for specific actions such as an explanation from the departmental manager.

A first-stage questionnaire might include such questions as, 'How satisfied are you with:

- the response of sales staff
- the location and convenience of the sales outlet
- convenience of opening hours
- ease of parking
- availability of product information
- product knowledge of staff
- waiting time to be served
- choice of payment methods
- explanation of options
- presentation of product
- availability of finance
- explanation of aftercare?'

The questionnaire which followed up at six months or a year after purchase would focus on customer satisfaction with the product or service and the quality of aftercare. It might include questions such as, 'How satisfied are you with:

- the quality and performance of the product
- the reliability of the product
- the benefits of the service
- the standard of the service
- the response of the branch to any queries
- the value of any instruction manuals
- the quality of after-care service
- the standard and speed of after-care
- the value of the warranty
- the availability of replacement parts

- the flexibility of service plans
- the availability of accessories?'

The two types of questionnaire are designed to assess how much effort staff are putting into selling the product properly, i.e. does the customer believe the staff is trying to help him or her select the right product. The answers to the questions can be used to assess the performance of the salesforce and the quality of product information. The questions on convenience can also act as a guide to the convenience of the sales outlet and help to plan changes or improvements.

The second questionnaire seeks to find out how well staff are faring during the critical period after the sale. It reminds the customer that there is life after the sale and helps to build contact during the critical period between sales when the customer could easily be influenced by offers from another manufacturer. If the customer is satisfied with all aspects of the company's service – product, convenience, quality and aftercare – it is likely that the customer will return for his next purchase.

RESPONDING TO SURVEYS

If surveys indicate low levels of satisfaction, the company has an opportunity to take remedial action or to respond to the customer's concerns. The real importance of a customer satisfaction index is whether it generates action and improves business performance. The index must be carefully weighted to focus the attention of the company on the key indicators of customer satisfaction. Each response is given a score and the totals of all customer responses are added up to give an overall index for the outlet. The index may be based on the answers to all questions or it may be based on a selection of questions which are most important to overall satisfaction.

Car dealerships, for example, concentrate on the response to after-care, 'How satisfied were you with the service from the Parts and Service departments?' because they know that the key to retaining customers between new car sales is the two to three-year period when the customer deals with the Parts and Service departments. One European manufacturer calculated that the new car sales process generated a possible 1 million contacts per year, while after-care generated a potential 5 million contacts. It was vital that their after-care programmes were perceived well by the customer.

This pattern will vary by type of purchase:

- In fast-moving consumer goods, for example, purchasing frequency is much higher; after-care would play a minor role in customer satisfaction, while

convenience, quality of checkout service, price, choice, parking, and opening hours would be more crucial.
- In the marketing of complex business-to-business products and services, the quality of advice and guidance, the level of pre-sales and after-sales support, and the contribution of other key long-term customer services are crucial factors which determine how well customers may benefit.

CUSTOMER SATISFACTION GUIDES

The customer satisfaction index, by itself, has little value. It gives an indication of how customers rate performance and provides a method of comparison, but unless companies take action to build on their strengths or improve their weaknesses, the questionnaire will be wasted. When a department or group is participating in a customer satisfaction programme, they should be given a programme guide outlining the reasons for the programme, the business benefits, and the actions they must take as a result of the programme.

Ford's customer satisfaction programme guide is a comprehensive publication aimed at the dealer principal and the dealership management team. It covers:

- the importance of customer satisfaction
- the scope of the programme
- the survey which is the basis of the programme
- the reasons for the questions
- the method of calculating the index
- the management actions that should be taken in response to the questionnaire
- a department-by-department guide to key customer concerns that have already been identified
- a summary of actions that other dealers have taken to meet those concerns
- a development programme for the dealership
- the training and business programmes available to improve customer satisfaction performance.

The most important sections are the management actions and the departmental guides. A customer satisfaction index is simply a starting-point for building a business that is focused on the customer. The programme manual recommends a series of meetings:

- a fortnightly review of all the responses received from customers during the previous period – all questionnaires are returned to a handling agency who analyse the responses and forward results and requests for action to individual dealerships once a fortnight

- a monthly review of action taken in response to the questionnaire
- a quarterly review of improvements in individual areas and in overall customer satisfaction.

At the fortnightly meetings, departmental managers are given the results of the previous questionnaire and asked to respond to any immediate requests from customers or to deal with any serious complaints within the questionnaires. If, for example, a customer says that they are extremely dissatisfied with a 36,000-mile service, the service manager will be told to contact the customer immediately to find out more information and make an immediate response.

The monthly meetings should focus on more general concerns. If, for example, a large number of customers say they are dissatisfied with parking arrangements or length of time spent in customer reception, the dealership can take action to improve the situation.

The quarterly meeting is a more formal review of progress in improvements and trends in customer satisfaction performance. The dealer principal should take the opportunity to review current improvement projects and to assess whether earlier improvement programmes have had a direct effect on overall customer satisfaction performance levels.

The departmental guides within the customer satisfaction manual are intended to give individual departments a clearer indication of their contribution to customer satisfaction and outline the actions they can take to improve performance. In a questionnaire on standards of service, for example, customers commented on grease marks on their car, cigarettes in the ashtray, radios tuned to a different frequency, or a fault recurring despite the service.

These comments, taken from actual questionnaires, demonstrated to members of staff who don't normally meet customers that there are good reasons for concentrating on customer care, and they show that the department's contribution is important. The section also includes practical examples of what other dealers have done to improve performance in this area. This helps dealers to put together their own action plans.

The customer satisfaction performance guide can be a valuable method of implementing customer care programmes within a local outlet, but it must be an action-oriented programme which local managers can put into immediate use.

CUSTOMER SATISFACTION INCENTIVE SCHEMES

The other value of a customer satisfaction index is that it can be used to encourage improvement using recognition and incentive programmes. By providing a quantitive basis for comparison, different departments or outlets around the country can compete with each other to demonstrate that they offer the highest levels of satisfaction. This competitive element can be used in a number of ways:

- to give incentive to local outlets to improve their own performance on a year-on-year basis
- to give incentive to individual outlets to improve their own performance
- to encourage the highest standards of customer satisfaction.

The incentive programmes should be based, not just on current performance, but on improvement and it must continue to recognise improvement over a long period of time. An extreme version of the incentive programme links local customer satisfaction performance to levels of investment – if an outlet does not achieve targets for customer satisfaction it may not qualify for investment or it may have its own operations restricted. Most programmes however recognise improvement and they can be based on regional or national groupings.

Top-performing outlets in a league receive an award or a prize. A higher status of award can be given to the outlets who achieve the very highest levels of customer satisfaction. A number of programmes operating under the banner of a chairman's or president's award recognise excellence in customer satisfaction with a special award for an élite group of branches. Ford's Chairman's Award is an élite pan-European award given to the top dealers in each of 16 territories; they are taken to a top European destination where they are personally recognised by the chairman of Ford of Europe. Programmes like this help to maintain the impetus of customer care programmes; they ensure that individual departments and outlets aim at continually improving standards.

BENEFITS OF THE PROGRAMME

Customer satisfaction performance programmes help companies implement programmes for measuring customer service standards. The measures reflect customer concerns and are based on customer responses. Because customers are involved in the process of measuring and improving customer service, relationships are strengthened. Customer satisfaction measurement and reward programmes can be focused on critical business activities so that the programmes can be used selectively. Where the programmes are used over a long period of time they can help to build increasingly higher standards of customer satisfaction.

KEY MANAGEMENT ACTIONS

- Identify the factors that should be measured using customer focus standards as a guide.
- Identify the individuals, departments or outlets that should be measured.
- Decide on the frequency of measurement.
- Launch the programme with a staff guide that explains the importance of the programme.
- Report on the measurements regularly to the target groups.
- Ensure that the groups respond to poor performance and implement improvement programmes.
- Recognise and reward exellence in customer satisfaction.

SUMMARY

This chapter has shown the importance of measuring customer satisfaction through customer surveys, and customer comments can be used to compile customer satisfaction guides. Finally, the chapter has shown how incentive and recognition schemes can be used to motivate local staff to achieve increasingly higher standards of customer satisfaction.

Self-assessment checklist

- Do you have formal procedures for measuring customer satisfaction?
- Are there common elements of customer satisfaction that work across international markets?
- Do your measures allow you to compare outlets across the network and departments within individual outlets?
- Do you set progressive customer satisfaction targets and reward improvement?
- How often do you measure customer satisfaction and how often do you provide reports to your local outlets?
- Is there a procedure for acting on customer satisfaction ratings?
- Are your surveys measuring the right factors and are some factors more important than others?

- Do you help local outlets to improve their customer satisfaction performance with training and recognition schemes?

- Can you tie customer satisfaction ratings to other performance factors to exert greater control over local performance?

- Is customer satisfaction treated as a priority in all your territories?

26

MEASURING SERVICE WITH QUALITY STANDARDS

Quality is increasingly used as a means of measuring standards of customer service. Quality standards can be applied and adapted to different types of business. Quality standards must be measurable; they should be carefully controlled and, ideally, they should conform to the standards of an independent organisation such as the British Standards Institute (BSI). BSI manage a broad range of standards for products and services. Product standards, for example, mean that products have been manufactured and inspected to extremely strict specifications and customers can feel confident that any batch of products coming from one company or from a number of sources will be consistent.

THE IMPORTANCE OF SERVICE MEASUREMENT

Service measurement and feedback are important in a number of scenarios:

- when a company is operating through a number of different outlets and wants to offer consistent standards through every outlet
- when services are critical to a customer's business success and quality measurement provides a competitive advantage
- when a company wants to demonstrate high levels of customer care.

MEASURING THE QUALITY OF LOCAL SERVICE

Quality techniques are now being applied to the standards of service available from a company and BS 5750 is the recognised means of demonstrating that a business conforms to international quality standards in the way it deals with customers. BS 5750 is not a set of rigid standards applied in the same way to every business; the business is measured in a number of different fields that are crucial to the quality of customer service. So BS 5750 would be applied in a different way to a manufacturing company and to a professional services consultancy. Each company is measured and can be compared easily and realistically.

Local performance can therefore be included in the scope of BS 5750. A group of solicitors, for example, who operated a network of local branches decided that it would be worth registering under BS 5750 to demonstrate that they were capable of delivering a quality professional service. The initial assessment was used to identify the critical activities which determined the successful operation of the practice. The assessment covered general activities such as speed of response to telephone and written enquiries, and more specific activities such as time spent in handling conveyancing or searches. Consultants worked with the practice management team to define a unique set of standards and to identify the actions that would be needed to achieve that standard in each of the branches.

The consultants drew up a timetable for achieving the standards and, when the practice had achieved them, it was awarded BS 5750. The process did not stop there because each branch had to continue to meet the performance standards to retain its status as a BS 5750 supplier. The practice was able to control the performance of each of its branches and was able to offer its clients a measurable standard of service.

MEASURING CUSTOMER SERVICE

BS 5750 is also at the heart of ICL's Customer Response Strategy which provides a central point of contact for customer enquiries throughout the country. Customer response was previously handled by individual branches dealing with their local customers, but branches did not necessarily have the skills or resources needed to deal with the full range of enquiries. The Customer Response Strategy is based on a Customer Reception Centre which is accessible 24 hours a day at local rates and provides a control centre for providing the customer with the right response. The Customer Reception Centre can draw on various ICL centres of excellence and co-ordinate their activities, keeping the customer fully informed on all aspects of the service.

The Customer Reception Centre, which appears to the customer to be a local branch response, conforms to BS 5750 and provides customers with a quality response to all their queries. Customer reception staff are measured on how quickly they reply to the original call, how quickly they provide a response within specific guidelines and how frequently they keep the customer informed until the task is completed. There is also an integral escalation procedure so that any queries that cannot be handled within target times are immediately handed on to other people within the organisation who have the authority to commit additional resources to the problem. ICL has solved the problem of consistent branch service by handling enquiries centrally, but the programme frees branch staff to carry out more proactive customer care work.

CONSISTENT LOCAL QUALITY

BS 5750 is also finding its way into the local service station; a number of Volvo and BMW dealerships, for example, now have service departments which conform to BS 5750 and this provides service customers with a reassurance of quality. Service technicians have always followed the guidelines of manufacturer's approved service schedules, but the new requirements of BS 5750 have added additional inspection processes and different work practices which improve the quality of the service department.

For example, incomplete jobs which might be waiting for replacement parts are labelled 'process incomplete' so that the vehicle is not accidentally moved while it is in a possibly dangerous condition. Other aspects of BS 5750 relate to the time taken to complete jobs, presentation and explanation of invoices and procedures for dealing with customer complaints. This improved quality of service and the seal of approval of an independent organisation helped to enhance the reputation of an area of the motor trade that has traditionally suffered from a poor reputation and it also enables the manufacturer to offer customers a consistent standard of service throughout the branch network.

MEASURING CUSTOMERS' EXPECTATIONS OF QUALITY

BSI registration provides an independent method of assessing and maintaining the quality of branch performance. Quality can also be assessed in line with customers' expectations of the service. Research into customers' attitudes shows how customers feel about the service that is being delivered. For example, many service organisations provide a questionnaire to customers at the end of every service asking how they rated different aspects of the service. The service engineers are also asked to complete a visit report describing the nature of the problem, the actions they took and the time taken to complete different aspects of the job. By analysing this information and comparing the performance of individual branches and individual engineers, the company can build up a profile of service performance and can take appropriate action to deal with any of the problems.

The performance survey covers such aspects as:

- time to reach customer
- promptness of arrival
- time to diagnose
- availability of replacement parts
- time to complete the task
- satisfaction with the standard of work
- helpfulness of the service engineer.

The fact that part of the measurement is based on actual customer assessment rather than a set of arbitrary standards provides greater credibility to the results and enables them to be presented as part of a customer focus programme. The customer surveys also provide an opportunity to maintain proactive communication with customers by showing that local outlets respond to customer queries and concerns. Chapter 11, Customer contact strategies, explains this process in more detail.

Measuring performance in quality is however only the starting point for achieving consistency. The customer surveys and the quality assessment indicate the key factors to be measured and the level of current achievement. The challenge to the supplier is how to raise and maintain the quality of performance throughout the local network.

MEASURING FEEDBACK

It is important that you obtain regular feedback from your customers to ensure that you are achieving the right level of customer satisfaction. Consultation on new product developments or participation in liaison committees and user groups allows you to take account of your customers' views, while effective complaints procedures demonstrate that you can deal with problems and respond effectively. There are many other ways of obtaining feedback using techniques such as:

- customer satisfaction surveys
- service cards
- telephone surveys
- review meetings.

BENEFITS OF THE PROGRAMME

By utilising quality-driven measurements, a company can impose consistent performance standards on different groups and outlets. Quality standards provide an independent form of measurement that ensures a valid means of comparison. By utilising customer feedback mechanisms, it is possible to focus improvement on customers' needs.

KEY MANAGEMENT TASKS

- Identify the tasks to be measured.
- Determine the measures to be used.
- Utilise independent quality measurements wherever possible.
- Introduce feedback mechanisms.
- Respond to poor results and implement improvement programmes.

SUMMARY

Quality techniques can be applied to the measurement and control of customer service as a means of monitoring performance and improving standards. Quality standards provide a valuable competitive differentiator and demonstrate a commitment to customer service. It is important to apply quality standards to customer-facing tasks and to involve customers in assessing performance.

Self-assessment checklist

- What are the critical customer-facing activities and how can they be measured?
- Can independent quality standards be used to measure performance?
- Can you use customer feedback techniques such as service questionnaires or telephone follow up to measure customer attitudes?
- Do you build improvement mechanisms into your measurement programmes?

27

SUMMARY

Customer focus is taking its place as one of the key business processes of the nineties. The techniques have changed from an initial emphasis on personal service by a small number of specialists to a company-wide focus on the customer that embraces business processes as well as personal skills. Technology is increasingly being used to enhance the quality of service to customers and to develop new ways of doing business which focus on customers' individual needs.

This book has given examples of a wide range of individual projects that can be used to tackle specific aspects of customer service appropriate to different companies. Underlying all the projects is a need to understand what the customer needs and without a commitment to continuous customer focus, individual programmes will only be short-term fixes. Customer-focused companies profit because they take a long-term view of customer relationships.

INDEX

Further titles of interest

FINANCIAL TIMES

PITMAN PUBLISHING

ISBN	TITLE	AUTHOR
0 273 60561 5	Achieving Successful Product Change	Innes
0 273 03970 9	Advertising on Trial	Ring
0 273 60232 2	Analysing Your Competitor's Financial Strengths	Howell
0 273 60466 X	Be Your Own Management Consultant	Pinder
0 273 60168 7	Benchmarking for Competitive Advantage	Bendell
0 273 60529 1	Business Forecasting using Financial Models	Hogg
0 273 60456 2	Business Re-engineering in Financial Services	Drew
0 273 60069 9	Company Penalties	Howarth
0 273 60558 5	Complete Quality Manual	McGoldrick
0 273 03859 1	Control Your Overheads	Booth
0 273 60022 2	Creating Product Value	De Meyer
0 273 60300 0	Creating World Class Suppliers	Hines
0 273 60383 3	Delayering Organisations	Keuning
0 273 60171 7	Does Your Company Need Multimedia?	Chatterton
0 273 60003 6	Financial Engineering	Galitz
0 273 60065 6	Financial Management for Service Companies	Ward
0 273 60205 5	Financial Times Guide to Using the Financial Pages	Vaitilingam
0 273 60006 0	Financial Times on Management	Lorenz
0 273 03955 5	Green Business Opportunities	Koechlin
0 273 60385 X	Implementing the Learning Organisation	Thurbin
0 273 03848 6	Implementing Total Quality Management	Munro-Faure
0 273 60025 7	Innovative Management	Phillips
0 273 60327 2	Investor's Guide to Emerging Markets	Mobius
0 273 60622 0	Investor's Guide to Measuring Share Performance	Macfie
0 273 60528 3	Investor's Guide to Selecting Shares that Perform	Koch
0 273 60704 9	Investor's Guide to Traded Options	Ford
0 273 03751 X	Investor's Guide to Warrants	McHattie
0 273 03957 1	Key Management Ratios	Walsh
0 273 60384 1	Key Management Tools	Lambert
0 273 60259 4	Making Change Happen	Wilson
0 273 60424 4	Making Re-engineering Happen	Obeng
0 273 60533 X	Managing Talent	Sadler
0 273 60153 9	Perfectly Legal Competitor Intelligence	Bernhardt
0 273 60167 9	Profit from Strategic Marketing	Wolfe
0 273 60170 9	Proposals, Pitches and Beauty Parades	de Forte
0 273 60616 6	Quality Tool Kit	Mirams
0 273 60336 1	Realising Investment Value	Bygrave
0 273 60713 8	Rethinking the Company	Clarke
0 273 60328 0	Spider Principle	Linton
0 273 03873 7	Strategic Customer Alliances	Burnett
0 273 03949 0	Strategy Quest	Hill
0 273 60624 7	Top Intrapreneurs	Lombriser
0 273 03447 2	Total Customer Satisfaction	Horovitz
0 273 60201 2	Wake Up and Shake Up Your Company	Koch
0 273 60387 6	What Do High Performance Managers Really Do?	Hodgson

For further details or a full list of titles contact:

The Professional Marketing Department, Pitman Publishing, 128 Long Acre, London WC2E 9AN, UK
Tel +44 (0)71 379 7383 or fax +44 (0)71 240 5771